# 2004
# NCAA M
# AND WO
# SOCCER RULES





**NATIONAL COLLEGIATE ATHLETIC ASSOCIATION**

[ISSN 0735-0368]

THE NATIONAL COLLEGIATE ATHLETIC ASSOCIATION

P.O. Box 6222

Indianapolis, Indiana 46206-6222

317/917-6222

www.ncaa.org

May 2004

**Manuscript Prepared By:** C. Cliff McCrath, *Secretary-Rules Editor, NCAA Men's and Women's Soccer Rules Committee.*

**Edited By:** Christina M. Schluep, *Assistant Director of Publishing.*

**Production/Design By:** Toi Davis, *Production Designer II.*



NCAA 18322-5/04

# Contents

# NCAA Men's and Women's Soccer Rules Committee

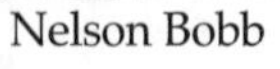

Nelson Bobb

C. Cliff McCrath

Lee Ellis

Gary Hamill

Steve Holeman

Stacy Lamb

James Phillips

Robert Russo

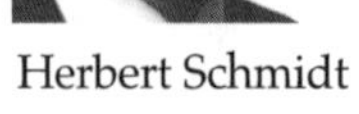

Herbert Schmidt

Kim T. Sutton

| Div. | | Term Expires |
|---|---|---|
| I | **Chair:** Steve Holeman<br>University of Mississippi, University, Mississippi 38677<br>Phone: 662/915-7859 Fax: 662/915-5648<br>E-mail: sholeman@olemiss.edu | 9-1-06 |
| II | **Secretary-Rules Editor:** C. Cliff McCrath<br>Seattle Pacific University, Seattle, Washington 98119<br>Phone: 206/281-2968 Fax: 206/281-2266<br>E-mail: cmccrath@spu.edu | 9-1-11* |
| III | Lee Ellis<br>Principia College, Elsah, Illinois 62028<br>Phone: 618/374-5030 Fax: 618/374-5221<br>E-mail: lee@prin.edu | 9-1-06 |
| II | Gary Hamill<br>Wingate University, Wingate, North Carolina 28174<br>Phone: 704/233-8175 Fax: 704/233-8170<br>E-mail: hamill@wingate.edu | 9-1-07 |
| I | Stacy Lamb<br>University of Louisiana-Monroe, Monroe, Louisiana 71209<br>Phone: 318/342-5090 Fax: 318/342-3594<br>E-mail: lamb@ulm.edu | 9-1-06 |
| I | James Phillips<br>Notre Dame University, Notre Dame, Indiana 46556<br>Phone: 574/631-5746 Fax: 574/631-9229<br>E-mail: phillips.71@nd.edu | 9-1-08 |
| III | Robert Russo<br>Denison University, Granville, Ohio 43023<br>Phone: 740/587-5735 Fax: 740/587-5362<br>E-mail: russo@denison.edu | 9-1-07 |
| I | Herbert Schmidt<br>Pennsylvania State University, University Park, Pennsylvania 16802<br>Phone: 814/863-3489 Fax: 814/863-8569<br>E-mail: whsl@psu.edu | 9-1-07 |
| II | Kim T. Sutton<br>California State University, Chico, California 95929-0300<br>Phone: 530/898-6085 Fax: 530/898-4699<br>E-mail: ktsutton@csuchico.edu | 9-1-04 |

**For all interpretations regarding rules, contact secretary-rules editor C. Cliff McCrath, Seattle Pacific University, 3307 3rd Avenue West, Seattle, Washington 98119; phone: 206/281-2968; fax: 206/281-2266; cell: 206/963-9047; e-mail: cmccrath@spu.edu.**

*Members who attended annual meeting but whose terms expired September 1, 2004:*
Nelson Bobb, University of North Carolina, Greensboro
Kim T. Sutton, California State University, Chico

# Major Rules Changes for 2004

*The figures below refer to rule and section respectively.*
*Each changed or altered segment is identified in the rules by a screened background.*

# Points of Emphasis

In each edition of the NCAA Men's and Women's Soccer Rules, there are several areas that are given special attention. These are identified as points of emphasis. While they may not represent any rules changes as such, their importance must not be overlooked. In some cases, the points of emphasis are more important than some of the rules changes. When a topic is included in the points of emphasis, there has been evidence during the previous year that there has been inconsistency in administering the rule.

Points of emphasis are accentuated with a frame around the specific rule within the main text of the rules book.

The figures below refer to the rule and section of those points the rules committee has decided to emphasize for the 2004 season.

## Governing Sports Authority Language

References to game authority or governing sports authority throughout the book generally refer to athletics directors of the participating institutions, conference commissioners or any other office that has jurisdiction over the game in question. **Governing Sports Authorities may not alter the rules of conduct as stated in this book (e.g., rescinding violations and misconduct rules before, during and after a contest and altering overtime procedures to accommodate a conferences post-season tournament).** For NCAA championships, the NCAA games committee is the game authority.

The NCAA Men's and Women's Soccer Rules have been designated as either administrative or conduct rules. Typically, administrative rules are those dealing with preparation for competition. They may be altered by **prior written mutual consent** of the competing institutions. Conduct rules are those that pertain directly to the competition. These rules may not be changed by mutual consent. All NCAA member institutions are required to conduct their intercollegiate contest according to these rules.

In the 2004 Men's and Women's Soccer rules, the administrative rules are Rules 1-1-b, 1-12-b, 1-13, 1-14, 1-15, 1-16, 4-1-c, 5-3-b, 6-5, 10-2, 10-3, 10-4, 10-5, 10-6. All other rules are conduct rules.

All references in the rules book to reports required to be filed by the referee refer to **written** reports that must be dispatched within 48 hours after the completion of the game to which the report relates. (***Exception:*** Referees must fax, telephone or electronic mail a fighting report immediately after the game.)

**For all interpretations regarding rules, contact secretary-rules editor C. Cliff McCrath, Seattle Pacific University, 3307 3rd Avenue West, Seattle, Washington, 98119; phone: 206/281-2968; fax: 206/281-2266; cell: 206/963-9047; e-mail: cmccrath@spu.edu.**

# RULE 1

# The Field of Play

### Dimensions

SECTION 1. a. The field of play shall be rectangular, the width of which shall not exceed the length.

b. The width shall not be more than 80 yards [73.15m] nor less than 65 yards [59.44m] and the length shall not be more than 120 yards [109.73m] nor less than 110 yards [100.58m]; however, fields of less than minimal dimensions may be used by prior written mutual consent of the competing institutions. The optimum size is 75 yards [68.58m] by 120 yards [109.73m]. Facilities constructed after September 1995 must be a minimum of 70 yards [64.01m] in width by 115 yards [105.15m] in length. (Exception: Facilities with architectural plans dated before September 30, 1995.)

It is the responsibility of the home team to notify the visiting team —- before the date of the game — of any changes in field dimensions (e.g., greater or lesser than minimal requirements), playing surface (e.g., from grass to artificial or vice versa) or location of the playing site. Further, it is recommended that teams agree on field dimensions before confirming contests or signing game contracts.

*Note: Rule 1-1-b is an administrative rule and may be altered by prior written mutual consent.*

**PENALTY—The game shall not begin and the referee shall file a report with the governing sports authority (see page 8).**

### Boundary Lines

SECTION 2. The field shall be marked with distinctive lines, in accordance with the diagram on page 10, the longer boundary lines being called the touch lines and the shorter the goal lines. The home team is responsible for the proper marking of the field.

The lines shall meet at the corners; that is, the goal lines shall extend completely across the field of play, including the area between the goal posts,

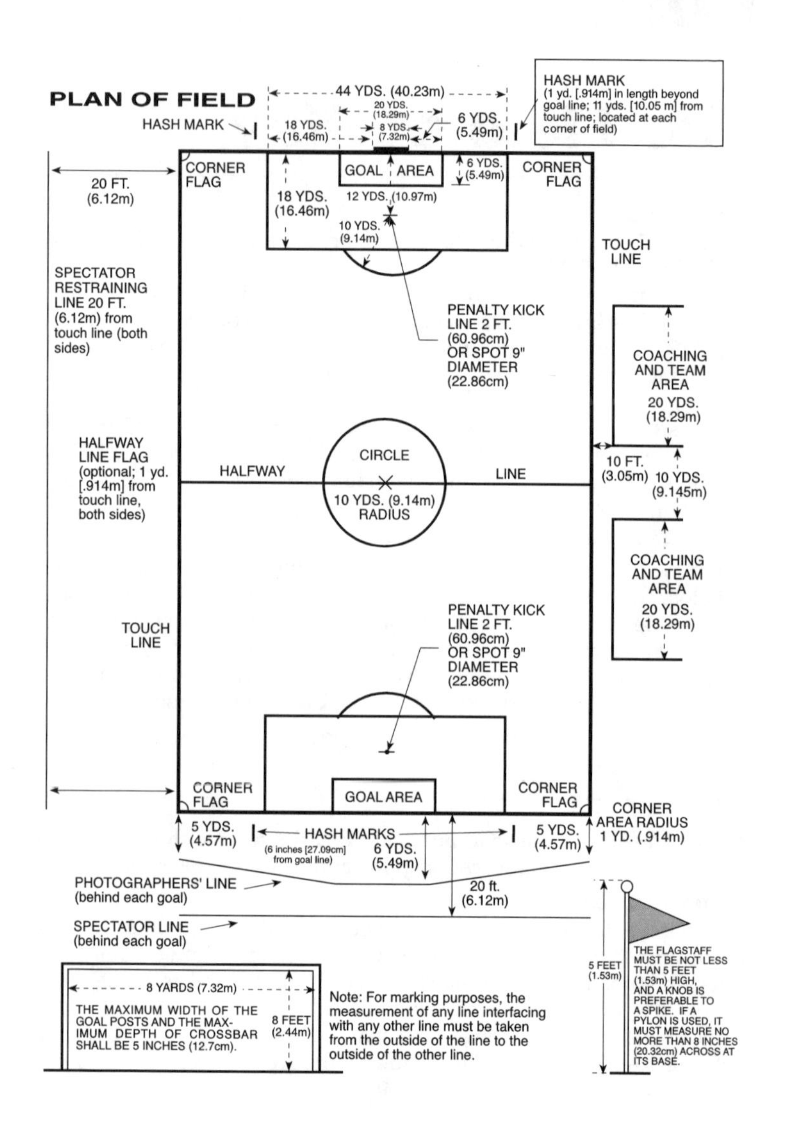
PLAN OF FIELD
44 YDS. (40.23m)
20 YDS. (18.29m)
HASH MARK
18 YDS. (16.46m)
8 YDS. (7.32m)
6 YDS. (5.49m)
HASH MARK
(1 yd. [.914m] in length beyond goal line; 11 yds. [10.05 m] from touch line; located at each corner of field)
20 FT. (6.12m)
CORNER FLAG
GOAL AREA
6 YDS. (5.49m)
CORNER FLAG
18 YDS. (16.46m)
12 YDS. (10.97m)
10 YDS. (9.14m)
TOUCH LINE
SPECTATOR RESTRAINING LINE 20 FT. (6.12m) from touch line (both sides)
PENALTY KICK LINE 2 FT. (60.96cm) OR SPOT 9" DIAMETER (22.86cm)
COACHING AND TEAM AREA
20 YDS. (18.29m)
HALFWAY LINE FLAG (optional; 1 yd. [.914m] from touch line, both sides)
HALFWAY
CIRCLE
LINE
10 YDS. (9.14m) RADIUS
10 FT. (3.05m)
10 YDS. (9.145m)
COACHING AND TEAM AREA
20 YDS. (18.29m)
TOUCH LINE
PENALTY KICK LINE 2 FT. (60.96cm) OR SPOT 9" DIAMETER (22.86cm)
CORNER FLAG
GOAL AREA
CORNER FLAG
5 YDS. (4.57m)
HASH MARKS
(6 inches [27.09cm] from goal line)
6 YDS. (5.49m)
5 YDS. (4.57m)
CORNER AREA RADIUS 1 YD. (.914m)
PHOTOGRAPHERS' LINE (behind each goal)
20 ft. (6.12m)
SPECTATOR LINE (behind each goal)
8 YARDS (7.32m)
THE MAXIMUM WIDTH OF THE GOAL POSTS AND THE MAXIMUM DEPTH OF CROSSBAR SHALL BE 5 INCHES (12.7cm).
8 FEET (2.44m)
Note: For marking purposes, the measurement of any line interfacing with any other line must be taken from the outside of the line to the outside of the other line.
5 FEET (1.53m)
THE FLAGSTAFF MUST BE NOT LESS THAN 5 FEET (1.53m) HIGH, AND A KNOB IS PREFERABLE TO A SPIKE. IF A PYLON IS USED, IT MUST MEASURE NO MORE THAN 8 INCHES (20.32cm) ACROSS AT ITS BASE.

and the touch lines shall extend the entire length of the field. All lines shall be clearly marked but may not be of a form (i.e., grooves, curbs or painted logos, designs or other permanent field markings) that could prove dangerous to players.

**PENALTY—The game shall not begin and the referee shall file a report with the governing sports authority (see page 8).**

### Field Markings and Measurements

SECTION 3. All lines, which are part of the areas they define, shall be no less than 4 inches [10.16cm] in width nor more than 5 inches [12.7cm] in width.

Measurements shall be taken from the outside of the line to the outside of the line with which it interfaces. However, when measuring the width of the goal and penalty areas, the measurements shall be taken from the inside of the goal post to the outside of the six- and 18-yard lines, respectively.

In the case of a field that is playable but on which, during the course of the game, the lines and markings have become invisible due to snow or other such conditions, the lines and markings shall be assumed to be present and decisions rendered accordingly (see Rule 5-5).

### Halfway Line, Center Circle

SECTION 4. A halfway line shall be marked out across the field of play. The center of the field shall be indicated by a suitable mark, and a circle with a 10-yard [9.14m] radius shall be marked around it.

**PENALTY—The game shall not begin and the referee shall file a report with the governing sports authority (see page 8).**

### Goal Area

SECTION 5. At each end of the field of play, two lines shall be drawn at right angles to the goal line, six yards [5.49m] from the inside of each goal post. These shall extend into the field of play for a distance of six yards [5.49m] and shall be joined by a line drawn parallel with the goal line. Each of the spaces enclosed by these lines and the goal line shall be called a goal area.

**PENALTY—The game shall not begin and the referee shall file a report with the governing sports authority (see page 8).**

### Penalty Area

SECTION 6. At each end of the field of play, two lines shall be drawn at right angles to the goal line, 18 yards [16.46m] from the inside of each goal post. These shall extend into the field of play for a distance of 18 yards [16.46m] and shall be joined by a line drawn parallel with the goal line. Each of the spaces enclosed by these lines and the goal line shall be called the penalty area.

At each end of the field, a two-foot [60.96cm] line or nine-inch [22.86cm] spot shall be placed at a point 12 yards [10.97m] from the midpoint of, and parallel to, the goal line. The line shall extend one foot [30.48cm] on either side of the undrawn center line. The spot shall be situated at a point 12 yards [10.97m] from the midpoint of, and parallel to, the goal line. The spot shall extend 4½ inches on either side of the undrawn center line. The penalty kick may be taken from any position on this line or spot.

Using the center of this penalty-kick line or spot, describe a 10-yard [9.14m] arc outside the penalty area and closing on the penalty area line. This is the restraining line for penalty kicks.

**PENALTY—The game shall not begin and the referee shall file a report with the governing sports authority (see page 8).**

### Corner Area, Hash Mark

SECTION 7. From each corner, a quarter circle, having a radius of one yard [.914m], shall be drawn inside the field of play. In addition, a hash mark one yard [.914m] in length, situated six inches beyond (but not touching) the field of play and 11 yards [10.05m] from the touch line shall be marked perpendicular to the goal line at each corner of the field (see Plan of Field, page 10).

**PENALTY—The game shall not begin and the referee shall file a report with the governing sports authority (see page 8).**

### Corner Flags

SECTION 8. A flag on a post not less than five feet [1.53m] high and having a nonpointed top shall be placed at each corner; a similar flagpost may be placed opposite the halfway line on each side of the field of play, at least one yard [.914m] outside the touch line.

The staff or post shall be approximately 1½ inches [3.81cm] thick and may be either round or square. The corner flag may not be removed for any purpose during the game. The flag shall be of some bright color, easily distinguishable from the surroundings, and shall be about two feet [60.96cm] long by one foot [30.48cm] wide and securely fastened to the post or staff.

The flagpost shall be implanted in the ground or shall rise from a pylon that measures no more than eight inches [20.32cm] across at its base, providing the post itself rises directly above the center of the intersection of the touch line and goal line.

**A.R. 1.** Upon inspecting the field, the referee discovers the absence of corner flags on the corner flagposts. RULING: The home team shall obtain appropriate flags for the corner flagposts. If unsuccessful, the game shall begin.

### Goals

SECTION 9. The goals shall be anchored, secured or counterweighted. The exterior edge of the goal post shall conform to the exterior edge of the goal line and shall consist of two wooden or metal posts, equidistant from the corner flags and eight yards [7.32m] apart (inside measurement), joined by a horizontal crossbar of similar material, the lower edge of which shall be eight feet [2.44m] from the ground.

The width or diameter of the goal posts and crossbar shall not be less than four inches [10.16cm] nor more than five inches [12.7cm]. The posts and crossbar may be square, rectangular, round or elliptical in shape, and shall be painted white.

In addition, no markings other than a single manufacturer's identification/logo of appropriate size may appear on the goal posts or the crossbar.

**PENALTY—The game shall not begin and the referee shall file a report with the governing sports authority (see page 8).**

### Goal Nets

SECTION 10. Nets shall be attached to the uprights and crossbars and secured behind each goal.

The goal nets shall be properly and firmly secured and put in order before every match, and care taken that there are no holes or possible openings for the escape of the ball. The nets shall be properly supported so that the top of the net will extend backward on a level with the crossbar for a distance of about two feet [.609m].

Nets may be multicolored; however, no markings other than a single manufacturer's identification/logo of appropriate size may appear on the net.

**PENALTY—The game shall not begin and the referee shall file a report with the governing sports authority (see page 8).**

**A.R. 2.** May a banner hang from a goal net? RULING: No.

**A.R. 3.** May goal nets be lettered or reflect school names, logos, slogans or any other commercial design? RULING: No.

### Displaced Crossbar

SECTION 11. If the crossbar becomes displaced during the game, play shall be suspended, and every effort shall be made to repair the crossbar. If, in the referee's opinion, it cannot be repaired within a reasonable period of time, or in a manner so as not to present a danger, the game shall not be resumed. A rope is not a satisfactory substitute for a crossbar. When the crossbar is replaced, the referee shall restart the game by dropping the ball where it was when play was suspended; or, if the ball was inside the goal area, it shall be dropped at the nearest point outside the goal area. If the ball was clearly in the possession of one team when play was suspended, play shall be restarted by an indirect free kick taken by that team.

### Coaching and Team Areas

SECTION 12. a. There shall be a coaching and team area. Team benches shall be on the same side of the field, separated by a 10-yard neutral zone, and shall be at least 10 feet [3.05m] (whenever possible) from the touch line. Coaches, players and bench personnel must remain inside their coaching and team area. ***Exception:*** Players warming up in preparation to enter the field of play are permitted to use the area which extends beyond their coaching and team areas.

b. Each coaching and team area should be marked parallel to the touch line and situated at least 10 feet [3.05m] from the touch line and extending 20 yards [18.29m] from the five-yard neutral zone measured from the halfway line in both directions.

*Note: Rule 1-12-b is an administrative rule and may be altered by prior written mutual consent.*

**PENALTY FOR IMPROPER MARKING—The game shall begin but the coach shall be reminded that in the future, proper markings are to be provided, and the referee shall file a report with the governing sports authority (see page 8).**

**PENALTY FOR BEING OUT OF COACHING AND TEAM AREA— The referee shall inform the offending coach that on a recurrence, an indirect free kick shall be awarded against the offending team from the point where the ball was when the infraction occurred. On the second infraction, a caution shall be issued. On the third infraction, an ejection shall be issued.**

**A.R. 4.** Are bench personnel in the press box permitted to communicate in any way with coaches in the coaching and team areas? RULING: No. Coaches and other bench personnel shall remain in their own coaching and team area.

### Photographers' Line

SECTION 13. There shall be a designated photographers' area (see Plan of Field, page 10).

*Note: Rule 1-13 is an administrative rule and may be altered by prior written mutual consent.*

### Timekeeper's Table

SECTION 14. If not using a press box for timekeeping, it is recommended that the timekeeper's table be placed on the same side of the field as the team benches, situated equidistant between the two team benches and at least 10 feet [3.05m] (whenever possible) from the touch lines.

*Note: Rule 1-14 is an administrative rule and may be altered by prior written mutual consent.*

### Spectator Restraining Line

SECTION 15. It is recommended that a rope, fence or some form of demarcation be used to keep spectators a minimum of 20 feet [6.10m] (whenever possible) away from the touch lines and goal lines.

*Note: Rule 1-15 is an administrative rule and may be altered by prior written mutual consent.*

### Scoreboard and Clock

SECTION 16. It is recommended that an electronically controlled clock and scoreboard, which can be seen by spectators and both benches, be provided and maintained in proper working order (see Rule 6-3).

*Note: Rule 1-16 is an administrative rule and may be altered by prior written mutual consent.*

# RULE 2

# The Ball

### Dimensions

SECTION 1. The circumference of the ball shall not be more than 28 inches [71.12cm] nor less than 27 inches [68.58cm]. The weight of the ball at the start of the game shall not be more than 16 ounces [454.4g] nor less than 14 ounces [397.6g], and the weight shall not exceed 16.75 ounces [475g] even when wet and used. The pressure of the ball shall be equal to 0.6 to 1.1 atmospheres at sea level. (It is recommended that the manufacturer indicate on the ball the recommended air pressure to meet the above standards.)

### Style, Shape and Material

SECTION 2. The ball shall be stitched and spherical. The outer casing shall be leather or approved synthetic and no material shall be used in its construction that might prove dangerous to players.

No fewer than three nor more than six balls shall be available for use in a game; the balls shall be identical in size, make, grade and color, and shall be furnished by the home team.

**PENALTY—The game shall not begin and the referee shall file a report with the governing sports authority (see page 8).**

**A.R. 5.** The ball becomes defective during play and the referee stops the game. How is the game restarted? RULING: If one team is in clear possession when the ball becomes defective, the ball is replaced and the game is restarted with an indirect free kick, subject to the restrictions of Rule 13-2. If one team is not in clear possession when the ball becomes defective, the game is restarted with a drop ball at that spot or at the nearest point outside the goal area.

# RULE 3

# Players and Substitutes

## Players

### Number of Players

SECTION 1. The game shall be played by two teams of 11 players each, one of whom shall be the goalkeeper. In addition, a minimum of seven players are required to start and finish a game.

**A.R. 6.** Team A starts with 10 players. May the 11th player join the team during a suspension of play? RULING: Yes, provided that the player is listed on the game roster, reports to the official scorer and is beckoned by the referee.

**A.R. 7.** A player is ejected before the start of a match. Must the team play with only 10 players? RULING: No, the team may begin the match with another player in place of the ejected player.

### Game Roster

SECTION 2. a. An official NCAA game roster, including the names and numbers of all players, coaches and other bench personnel, shall be submitted to the referee, official scorekeeper and opposing coach no later than 15 minutes before game time. The game roster submitted to the official scorekeeper and the opposing coach shall include each player's total number of cautions and ejections in the columns beside the players' names. In addition, the roster must include the name(s) and number(s) of the suspended player(s) and date(s) of the suspension(s). Further, the copy submitted to the referee shall not include each player's total number of cautions and ejections.

**PENALTY—The game shall not begin and may result in a forfeiture by the offending team to be determined by the governing sports authority (see page 8).**

b. Player(s) not listed on the game roster are not eligible to participate in that game, overtime period(s) or tie breaker.

c. It is recommended that once assigned, each player retain the same number throughout the season.

**PENALTY—The unlisted player, who may be replaced, shall be instructed to leave the game and is not eligible to participate in that game or overtime period or tiebreaker.**

**A.R. 8.** Is there a limit on the number of players allowed to dress for a game? RULING: No, unless restricted by the appropriate governing sports authority.

**A.R. 9.** A player has a total of six cautions. Is the number submitted on the game roster a six or a one? RULING: Six.

**A.R. 10.** In the event of any problems regarding participation in the game by ineligible players, is the referee required to submit a written report? RULING: Yes, a written report shall be filed with the game authority (see page 8).

**A.R. 11.** It is determined that a player(s) has not been listed on the game roster. RULING: Remove the player(s) from the game. Players not listed on the game roster are not eligible to play in that game.

**A.R. 12.** A player(s) on the game roster submitted by either team is ejected by the referee before the start of the game. May that player's name on the game roster be replaced with another player's name? RULING: Yes, provided it is done before the start of the game.

**A.R. 13.** It is determined that a goal is scored by a player not listed on the game roster. RULING: Provided it is determined before the end of the game, the player shall be removed from the game and the goal nullified.

**A.R. 14.** It is determined after the game has been completed that the name and/or number of a player was incorrect or omitted. RULING: The score stands. Neither the outcome nor the statistics in any completed contest are reversible due to postgame administrative actions.

**A.R. 15.** It is determined that a player's number is listed incorrectly on the official roster. RULING: The name and number of each player must be correctly listed on the official roster before the game begins. Provided the player's name is listed correctly on the game roster and the roster is corrected to reflect the proper number, the player is eligible to compete in the game.

**A.R. 16.** It is determined during an overtime period that a player not listed on the game roster scored a goal during regulation play. RULING: Nullify the goal, end the game and declare the opposing team the winner.

**A.R. 17.** A player scores a goal or makes an assist, and it is later determined that the player's number was listed incorrectly on the game roster. Does the goal count? RULING: Yes, providing the player's name is listed correctly on the game roster and the roster is corrected to reflect the proper number.

**A.R. 18.** A player is listed on the roster as having accumulated four cautions. The opposing coach insists that the player has a total of five cautions and should not be allowed to participate in that game. If the referee cannot get the opposing coach to agree, what action should the referee take? RULING: Start the game on time, allow the player to play and submit a written report to the game authority (see page 8).

## Substitutes

### Number of Substitutes

SECTION 3. Either team may substitute up to 11 players at a time under the conditions set forth in Rule 3-4.

### When Allowed

SECTION 4. Substitutes may enter the game under the following conditions:

a. On a goal kick;
b. On a team's own throw-in; [Note: If the team in possession chooses to substitute, providing the requisites of Rule 3-6 are met, the opposing team also may substitute up to 11 players at that time.]
c. On a team's own corner kick; [Note: If the team in possession chooses to substitute, providing the requisites of Rule 3-6 are met, the opposing team also may substitute up to 11 players at that time.]
d. After a goal has been scored;
e. Between periods;
f. When a player has been cautioned; [Note: In the case of a player(s) being cautioned, the coach may substitute for the player(s) cautioned. If such a substitution is made, the opponent shall have the opportunity to make an equal number of substitutions at that time.]
g. When a goalkeeper has been ejected; [Note: In the case of a goalkeeper being ejected, his or her team must play short, and the coach may substitute for the ejected goalkeeper only. If such a substitution is made, a field player must be removed, and the opposing team may not substitute at that time.]
h. When a player has been instructed to leave the field for an equipment change.

*[Note: In the event of an equipment change, only the player(s) with the equipment problem may be replaced. The opponent may replace an equal number of players at the same time.]*

i. In the event of an injury. [Note: In the event of an injury, only the injured player(s) may be replaced. The opponent may replace an equal number of players at the same time.]

**PENALTY—Indirect free kick for the nonoffending team from the location of the ball at the time the infraction is discovered if the reason for the stoppage of play was the infraction.**

**A.R. 19.** May a coach or other bench personnel communicate (i.e., provide coaching instruction) with his/her players while attending injured player(s) while on the field of play? RULING: No (see Rule 12-20).

**A.R. 20.** May a player who has been removed from the game for an equipment change return? RULING: Yes, if the player was not substituted for while completing the equipment change, the player may return. No, if another player was substituted for the player with the equipment change, the original player may not reenter the game in the period in which he or she was replaced. ***Exception:*** The player is allowed one reentry in the second period only.

**A.R. 21.** A player from Team A is injured and the coach sends in a substitute. At this point, Team B sends in two substitutes without the referee noticing it. RULING: After stoppage of play, the last Team B player to enter the game shall return to the bench. Caution the player and/or coach and award an indirect free kick to Team A from the location of the ball at the time the infraction was discovered. In addition, the "illegal" player is charged with a substitution.

**A.R. 22.** A player has been cautioned for misconduct. Before the kick is taken, may a player enter the game as a substitute for the cautioned player? RULING: Yes, and the opposing team may make an equal number of substitutions.

**A.R. 23.** If the goalkeeper is ejected and a field player is removed to allow a substitute goalkeeper to enter the game, is the field player charged with a substitution? RULING: Yes.

## Reentry Conditions, Restrictions, Exceptions

SECTION 5. With reference to periods of play, substitutions are permitted as follows:
First half: No reentry.
Second half: One reentry.
First overtime period: No reentry.
Second overtime period: No reentry.

*Exceptions:*

a. Goalkeepers—Unlimited reentry in all periods providing they reenter as goalkeepers and not as players in other positions.
b. Illness/Injury/Bleeding or Blood on Uniform—If a substitution is made: (1) Players whose injury was caused by an opposing player who was cautioned or ejected in conjunction with the injury may be substituted for and reenter the game in any period (after being beckoned by the referee) at any stoppage of play or at any of the allowable times for normal substitutions. Neither the injured player nor the substitute shall be charged with a substitution. (2) Players instructed to leave the field of play because of a bleeding injury or blood on the uniform may be substituted for and reenter the game (after being beckoned by the referee) at any stoppage of play or at any of the allowable times for normal substitution, providing the appropriate medical personnel have given clearance. Neither the injured player nor the substitute shall be charged with

a substitution. (***Exception:*** After a goal is scored or between periods, providing it is done in a timely manner, substitutes are not required to "be ready" before the period begins or the kick-off to restart the game.) (3) Players leaving the field of play for normal illness/injury may not reenter the game in that same period. ***Exception:*** Players are permitted one reentry in the second period only.

If a substitution is not made (team plays short): Players leaving the game for illness/injury may reenter the game (after being beckoned by the referee) during the run of play or at any stoppage of play, including times for normal substitutions.

**A.R. 24.** May a player who is replaced in the first overtime period reenter the game in the second overtime period? RULING: Yes.

**A.R. 25.** A player does not start the second half but later enters the game and subsequently is substituted for. May that player reenter the game in the second half? RULING: Yes.

**A.R. 26.** A player receives a caution but is not substituted for at the time of the caution. Play is restarted and later the cautioned player is replaced. May he or she be permitted to reenter the game in the same period? RULING: No. ***Exception:*** Players are permitted one reentry in the second period only.

**A.R. 27.** A player is cautioned and substituted for at the time of the caution. May the player reenter in that same period? RULING: No. ***Exception:*** Players are permitted one reentry in the second period only.

**A.R. 28.** An injured player is replaced in the second half, and an opposing player is cautioned or ejected as a result of the injury. The injured player(s) subsequently returns to the game in that half and later is substituted for again. Is he or she permitted one additional reentry? RULING: Yes.

**A.R. 29.** A player instructed to leave the field due to a bleeding injury or blood on the uniform is cleared to reenter the game in a given period. If the injury was not caused by an opponent who was cautioned or ejected at the time of the injury, is the player allowed to reenter the game with reference to Rule 3-5-b? RULING: Yes, and the player who enters the game as a substitute also is exempt from the rule and may reenter the game in the same half. However, if the injured player replaces a player other than the original substitute, that player shall be charged with a substitution.

### Reporting into the Game

SECTION 6. A substitute shall report to the scorekeeper's table (or nearest assistant referee if the official scorekeeper is in the press box), be ready to enter the game before the time when substitutions are allowed, remain at the scorekeeper's table (or near the halfway line) and be beckoned by the referee before entering the field of play. To facilitate substitutions, a noise-producing instrument with a distinctly different tone (a horn is suggested) from the referee's signaling device shall be provided. In addition, during the final five minutes of the second period only, the referee shall signal that the clock be stopped and beckon the substitute(s) onto the field. (See Rule 6-3-b-(1)-(e).)

Any player who has left the field of play with or without the referee's permission after a game has started shall not return to the field or participate in play without first receiving the referee's permission.

Any player who enters or leaves the field during the progress of the game, except through normal movement of play, without the referee's permission shall be guilty of misconduct.

**PENALTY—Caution the player and award an indirect free kick from the location of the ball at the time of the infraction.**

**A.R. 30.** Shall the referee also beckon a substitute(s) onto the field after the clock has been stopped? RULING: Yes.

**A.R. 31.** A player enters or reenters the field of play without first receiving the referee's permission. RULING: The player and/or coach shall be cautioned. If stoppage of play is necessary, the game shall be restarted with an indirect free kick by a player of the opposing team from the place where the ball was when the game was stopped.

**A.R. 32.** Must the player entering the game remain at the halfway line until the departing player exits the field? RULING: No. The player may enter the field when beckoned by the referee.

**A.R. 33.** Must the departing player exit the field at the halfway line? RULING: Yes, unless the departing player is injured and cannot leave the field unassisted.

**A.R. 34.** When does a substitute become a field player of record? RULING: During the first 85 minutes of the game and during both overtime periods: At the moment the referee beckons the player(s) onto the field. In the last five minutes of the second regulation period: When the referee signals the clock to be stopped.

**A.R. 35.** Does a player(s) have to enter the field of play after the referee has beckoned or signaled the clock to be stopped for a substitution(s)? RULING: No. However, the player(s) shall be charged with one substitution entry.

**A.R. 36.** Multiple players have reported to the scorekeeper (or assistant referee) to enter the game as substitutes. The referee beckons or signals to stop the clock (last five minutes of second period) and the coach decides to hold one player back. Is that player charged with a substitution entry? RULING: Yes.

## Changing Goalkeepers

SECTION 7. The referee shall be notified when a goalkeeping change is made, either by another player on the field changing places with the goalkeeper or by substitution from the team bench.

**PENALTY—Both players (goalkeepers) shall receive a verbal admonition at the next stoppage of play.**

**A.R. 37.** On a penalty kick, the coach decides to substitute goalkeepers. RULING: Illegal substitution.

**A.R. 38.** May a teammate already on the field change positions with the goalkeeper for the taking of a penalty kick? RULING: Yes, provided the referee is notified.

**A.R. 39.** May a teammate on the field of play change positions with the goalkeeper? RULING: Yes, provided it occurs during stoppage of play and all other rules pertaining to players' uniforms are satisfied (see Rules 4-2 and 4-3).

# RULE 4

# Players' Equipment

### Uniform

SECTION 1. a. A field player's uniform shall consist of a jersey or shirt, shorts, stockings and shoes (see Rule 4-4). Further, in accordance with NCAA Bylaw 12.5.5, an institution's uniform or any item of apparel (including warm-ups) that is worn by a student-athlete while representing the institution in intercollegiate competition may contain only a single manufacturer's or distributor's logo or trademark on the outside of the apparel (regardless of the visibility of the logo or trademark). The logo or trademark must be contained within a four-sided geometrical figure (i.e., rectangle, square, parallelogram) that does not exceed 2¼ square inches. Such an item of apparel may contain more than one manufacturer's or distributor's logo or trademark on the inside of the apparel provided the logo or trademark is not visible.

If an institution's uniform or any item of apparel worn by a student-athlete in competition contains washing instructions on the outside of the apparel or on a patch that also includes the manufacturer's or distributor's logo or trademark, the entire patch must be contained within a four-sided geometrical figure (i.e., rectangle, square, parallelogram) that does not exceed 2¼ square inches.

The restriction of the size of a manufacturer's or distributor's logo is applicable to all apparel worn by student-athletes during the conduct of the institution's competition, which includes any pregame or postgame activities such as pregame warm-ups, including individual player warm-up attire before entering the game, postgame celebrations or pre- or postgame press conferences involving student-athletes.

The logo restrictions on student-athletes' apparel set forth in Bylaw 12.5.5 apply during NCAA championships to all personnel (e.g., coaches, trainers, managers) who are on the team bench for practices and games and who participate in NCAA news conferences.

The same logo restrictions on student-athletes' apparel also shall apply to commercial logos on uniforms worn by band members, cheerleaders, dance team members and the institution's mascot during NCAA championship events.

A commemorative patch may be permitted on a jersey or shirt. The entire patch must be contained within a four-sided geometrical figure (i.e., rectangle, square, parallelogram) that does not exceed 2¼ square inches.

b. Players shall wear shinguards under the stockings in the manner intended, without exception. The shinguards shall be professionally manufactured, age and size appropriate and not altered to decrease protection.

c. It is recommended that a special armband (which shall be worn on the arm) be worn that distinguishes the team captain(s) from other players on his or her team.

*Note: Rule 4-1-c is an administrative rule and may be altered by prior written mutual consent.*

**Contrasting Colors**

SECTION 2. All players of a team must wear matching uniforms. It is the responsibility of the home team to wear jerseys and stockings in clear contrast to those worn by the visiting team.

Any visible garment worn under the jersey shall be a solid color that matches the dominant color of the jersey. Shorts may differ in color from that of the stockings and jerseys but shall be matching in color and uniform in style. Any visible garment worn under the jersey or shorts shall be a solid color that matches the dominant color of the respective garment.

Goalkeepers shall wear jerseys and socks that distinguish them from all field players and referees.

**Numbers Mandatory**

SECTION 3. Numerals at least eight inches [20.32cm] in height that are easily distinguishable from the predominant background color(s) and pattern shall be worn on the back of each player's (including goalkeeper's) jersey.

Numerals at least four inches [10.16cm] in height that are easily distinguishable from the predominant background color(s) and pattern shall be worn on the front of each player's (including goalkeeper's) jersey. The same number shall be displayed on both the front and back of the jersey, and no two teammates may wear the same number.

### Shoes

SECTION 4. Shoes must be worn by all participants in a game. Shoes with soles containing aluminum, leather, rubber, nylon or plastic cleats, studs or bars, whether molded as part of the sole or detachable, are allowed as long as the referee does not consider them dangerous.

### Articles

SECTION 5. A player shall not wear anything that is dangerous to any player.

Knee braces with any metal parts are permissible provided no metal is exposed. Casts are permissible if they are covered and the referee does not consider them dangerous. Headgear, headbands and hats (goalkeepers only) are legal providing they are not considered dangerous to any player.

It is mandatory that the referee examine the equipment of each player before each game to see that it complies with the foregoing standards. Prostheses may be worn as long as the equipment is well-padded to protect not only the affected player but also his/her opponents. Any such device with exposed rivets, pins, sharp edges or any form of exterior fastener that would present a hazard must be properly padded.

**A.R. 40.** A player is wearing articles considered dangerous. The coach insists that the player in previous games had been allowed to wear these articles and refuses to make the player take off the articles. RULING: The referee shall instruct the player to leave the field until he or she conforms to Rules 4-5 and 4-6.

**A.R. 41.** If a player was instructed to leave the field for not conforming to Rule 4-5, may that player return at any time after rectifying the problem? RULING: If the player was not substituted for, that player may reenter the game when the ball is not in play, after receiving approval from the referee (see Rules 3-4-h and 3-4-i). ***Exception:*** The player, if substituted for, may reenter in the second period only providing he or she had not previously reentered in that period.

**A.R. 42.** A player is wearing a cast or other article. RULING: Casts and other articles shall be inspected before the match (see Rule 4-5). The referee shall determine that the cast and other articles are not dangerous or the player(s) shall not be allowed to participate. Both coaches shall be informed of the referee's decision. If during the match the player is judged to be using properly covered articles as implements to gain an unfair advantage, or in a manner that might endanger any participant, the player shall not be allowed to continue in the match. However, the player ordered off the field for dangerous equipment may be substituted for at that time.

### Jewelry

SECTION 6. A player shall not wear any jewelry, including earrings, chains, charms, watches, hair clips, bobby pins, tongue studs or items associated with piercing (visible or not visible). ***Exception:*** Medical alert bracelets or necklaces may be worn but must be taped to the body.

**PENALTY—If the referee considers any article liable to cause injury to another player, including head, face or body protective equipment, the referee shall signal the clock to be stopped and instruct the player to leave the field of play and remove the illegal article. Any player not conforming to Sections 1 through 6 shall not be permitted to play. After being instructed to leave the field, providing he/she has not been substituted for, a player shall not reenter the game without first reporting to the referee, who shall be satisfied that the player's uniform, shoes and equipment are in order.**

**PENALTY—The referee stops the clock and the player shall leave the field of play. Once the player has complied, the player or a substitute may reenter at the next allowable substitution opportunity (see Rule 3-4).**

**A.R. 43.** A player, due to religious beliefs, is required to wear items (crosses, rosary beads, yarmulkes, etc.) not conforming to Sections 1 through 6. RULING: The referee shall use every discretion in attempting to enforce the rule but is obliged to follow the PENALTY set forth in Rule 4-5 if he or she considers the item(s) liable to cause injury to any player.

# RULE 5

# The Referee

### Number of Referees

SECTION 1. Either the dual or diagonal system of control may be used. However, the three-person, diagonal system of control (DSC) is preferred.

### Uniform

SECTION 2. All referees shall dress in the prescribed uniform and wear shoes that are predominantly black. Shirts of the same color and style shall be alike for all officials and shall be in contrast to those worn by the competing teams. It is permissible for officials to wear a cap.

### Jurisdiction

SECTION 3. a. The referee's jurisdiction shall begin 30 minutes before the start of play and shall end when the officials leave the site of the competition. The site of the competition is defined as the field, locker rooms, parking areas and the surroundings generally associated with athletics facilities.

The referee shall enforce the rules and decide any disputed point. The referee's decision is final so far as the result of the game is concerned.

The referee's power of penalizing shall extend to offenses committed when play has been suspended or when the ball is out of play. The referee shall, however, refrain from penalizing in cases where he or she is satisfied that by doing so an advantage would be given to the offending team. When the referee observes a foul that is not to be penalized, the referee shall call out the words "play on" and signal accordingly to indicate that the foul has been acknowledged. However, if the advantage does not materialize, the referee shall then blow the whistle and award a free kick.

When signaling, the referee shall use the "Official Referee Signals." (See diagrams at the back of the rules book.)

b. It is recommended that all officials remain on the field of play after the completion of the game until postgame duties have been completed.

*Note: Rule 5-3-b is an administrative rule and may be altered by prior written mutual consent.*

## Duties

SECTION 4. a. Pregame duties shall include: (1) Surveying field conditions (for safety purposes); (2) Inspecting the field markings; (3) Inspecting the goals and nets; (4) Inspecting the team benches and timekeeper's table (if located between team benches); (5) Inspecting corner flags; (6) Inspecting game balls; (7) Inspecting players' uniforms and equipment; and (8) Obtaining both team rosters. Violations involving field conditions, uniforms, equipment or other items shall be reported immediately to the appropriate authority and, if possible, necessary changes or repairs shall be made before the contest.

b. Postgame duties shall include signing the official NCAA box score and reporting ejections and other matters of game misconduct to the appropriate governing sports authority.

**A.R. 44.** Can a player be cautioned and/or ejected during an interval between periods or after the completion of a match? RULING: Yes. Moreover, if time remains and the player in question has not been substituted for before the incident occurs or the penalty has been assessed, the team shall play short for the remainder of the game.

**A.R. 45.** What action shall be taken when a referee fails to enforce a specific rule of conduct? RULING: The rule stated in the rules book shall be followed.

## Discretionary Power

SECTION 5. The referee has discretionary power to:

a. Suspend the game whenever, by reason of the elements (see lightning policy, Rule 10-10), interference by spectators or other cause, such action is deemed necessary. A suspended game may be resumed should conditions warrant. If the suspended game is not resumed, the referee shall file a report with the appropriate governing authority for later administrative action (see Rule 10-9).

b. Caution any player, coach or other bench personnel for misconduct or unsporting behavior (persistent infringement on any of the rules of the game) and, if the behavior persists, eject that individual from the game. When cautioning a player, coach or other bench personnel, the referee shall display a yellow card and indicate the appropriate person. If a previously cautioned player, coach or other bench personnel commits a second cautionable offense, the referee shall display a yellow card followed immediately by a red card. When ejecting a player, coach or other bench personnel, a red card shall be displayed. A player receiving a red card shall be ejected from the game and cannot be replaced. An ejected player, coach or other bench personnel shall leave the premises of the field of play to the point that the individual, in the referee's opinion, shall not be a disruptive influence on the further progress of the game. That usually means out of sight and sound of the field of play.

c. Forfeit the game to the opposing team if: (1) in his or her judgment, a coach prolongs a discussion with an official or refuses to leave the field at the request to do so; (2) a team refuses to return to the field of play within three minutes after being ordered to do so by the referee; and (3) a player ejected earlier in the game reentered the game as a substitute and is later detected as an illegal substitute.
d. Declare a "no contest" when a team without prior notification is not on the field and prepared to play within 15 minutes after the contracted starting time unless evidence of extenuating circumstances can be provided.
e. Suspend the game and stop the clock due to injury. (1) General injuries: If the player is not the goalkeeper, and medical personnel are beckoned to attend the player(s), the referee shall instruct the player(s) to leave or be removed from the field of play. Players leaving the game for illness or injury, providing they have not been replaced, may reenter the game (after being beckoned by the referee) during the run of play or at any stoppage of play, including times for normal substitutions. If the referee signals the clock to be stopped to assess a player's injuries and it is determined that medical personnel are not needed, the player(s) does not have to leave the field. (2) Bleeding, oozing injuries or blood on uniform: If necessary, summon medical personnel to escort or remove the player(s) from the field of play. The player(s) may reenter the game after the injury has been properly treated, the uniform has been evaluated by appropriate medical personnel for potential infectivity and changed, if necessary, before return to participation, and permission has been granted by the referee (see Rule 3-5).
f. Suspend the game and stop the clock when a player has been instructed to leave the field for an equipment change or jewelry violation.
g. Suspend the game, stop the clock and direct the game management personnel to remove artificial noisemakers, air horns, electronic amplifiers and any other items that are not permitted from the spectators areas.

**A.R. 46.** Multiple players appear to be injured in a single incident and medical personnel are beckoned onto the field of play. Do all players requiring medical attention have to leave the field of play? RULING: Yes, unless one of the players is a goalkeeper. The goalkeeper is allowed to remain.

**A.R. 47.** If the injured player is the goalkeeper, may the player remain in the game and be treated on the field of play? RULING: Yes.

**A.R. 48.** If a game is suspended by the referee because of the elements, interference by spectators, grave disorders or other causes, can a forfeit be declared? RULING: No, the referee has no authority to decide that either team is disqualified, unless specifically stated in Rule 5-5-c.

**A.R. 49.** The referee determines that spectators are interfering with the progress of the game. RULING: Spectators must stay in the seating areas or remain behind ropes, fencing or other barriers. In addition, photographers shall have freedom to operate in their prescribed areas. The referee has the right to stop the clock and instruct the host institution to remove spectators who do not comply.

**A.R. 50.** A player from Team B walks off the field without permission while the game is in progress, then walks back onto the field. RULING: Any player who leaves the field without permission, except through the normal course of play, is guilty of unsporting conduct.

**A.R. 51.** May a referee reverse a decision or rescind a card? RULING: Yes, if the game has not been restarted. No, if the game has been restarted.

**A.R. 52.** When may a referee reverse a decision involving a sudden-victory goal? RULING: Any time prior to signing the Official NCAA Box Score form or leaving the site of competition (see Rules 5-3-a and 6-4).

**A.R. 53.** A player commits two infringements of a different nature at the same time. RULING: The more serious offense shall be penalized.

**A.R. 54.** In the event the coach is ejected from the game and an institutional representative is unavailable to replace the coach for the balance of the game, what action is to be taken by the referee? RULING: Suspend the game.

**A.R. 55.** In the event the trainer is ejected from the game and no suitable certified medical authority or replacement is available, what action is to be taken by the referee? RULING: Ensure that the trainer is within a reasonable distance to be summoned in the event of an emergency.

**A.R. 56.** When a player is removed from the field as a result of an injury, shall the player be replaced by a substitute player? RULING: No. A team may continue play with fewer players. However, such action is unnecessary if the injury was caused by an opponent who was cautioned or ejected as a result of the injury, inasmuch as the injured player may reenter the game in the same period (see Rule 3-5-b).

**A.R. 57.** If an injured player is unable to return, may the replacement be given permission to enter the game at the next stoppage of play? RULING: Yes, and the opposing team may make appropriate substitutions in accordance with Rule 3-4-i.

**A.R. 58.** What happens in the event that the assigned referee fails to appear for a game? RULING: (1) The assistant referee with greater game experience shall assume the role of referee for that game. (2) Once the game begins, should the assigned referee then appear, that assistant referee still shall complete the game as referee. The assigned referee, who arrives after the start of play, may then step into the open assistant referee's position. (3) That assistant referee, who has to assume the role of referee, shall try to obtain the services of a certified referee to fill the open assistant referee's position, if immediately available. (4) Failing (3) above, that assistant referee shall try to obtain the services of a club assistant referee. A club assistant referee shall be limited to indicating when the ball is out of play. No other duties shall be assigned. (5) If no replacement is available for the missing official, the two assistant referees assigned to the game then shall operate the dual-referee system of game control.

**A.R. 59.** What happens in the event that an assigned assistant referee fails to appear for a game? RULING: (1) The assigned referee shall try to obtain the services of a certified referee to fill the open assistant referee position, if immediately available. (2) If no replacement is available for the missing official through (1), the assigned referee then shall operate the dual-referee system with the remaining referee (i.e., assigned assistant referee) serving as the second referee.

**A.R. 60.** The assigned officials for the game fail to appear. May that game be played? RULING: Yes, provided that both teams agree on the selection and use of replacement officials at that time.

# RULE 6

# Other Officials and Their Duties

### Assistant Referees

SECTION 1. Two assistant referees shall be appointed, whose duties (subject to the referee's decision and supervision) shall be to:

a. Indicate when the ball is out of play;
b. Indicate which side is entitled to a corner kick, goal kick or throw-in;
c. Indicate when a player may be penalized for being in an offside position;
d. Indicate when a substitution is desired; and
e. Assist the referee (subject to the referee's decision and supervision) to control the game in accordance with the rules by:
   (1) Indicating to the referee any breach of the rules that the referee may not have seen;
   (2) Helping with pregame and postgame duties, including (but not limited to) inspecting player equipment, field, game balls, game reports and other items;
   (3) Keeping track of the halftime interval, and notifying the referee and teams three minutes before the start of play; and
   (4) Giving an opinion on any point on which the referee may request.

### Alternate Official

SECTION 2. A conference or an institution may elect to assign an alternate official to a competition in order to assure game officiating continuity in the event one of the assigned officials is unable to perform his or her duties. When an alternate official is assigned, the game authority (see page 8) will clearly state the officiating position he or she will assume in the event that one of the referees or assistant referees is unable to officiate.

The alternate official is under the assigned referee's jurisdiction and performs duties that include: monitoring timekeeper and scorekeeper duties; managing substitutions and treatment of injuries; half-time checks; recording cautions and ejections; and assisting in control of bench personnel. The alternate official shall remain near the halfway line between the coaching and team areas during play.

**Timekeeper**

SECTION 3. When an electronically controlled scoreboard clock is visible to both benches and spectators, it shall be used as the official timepiece, and there shall be one official timekeeper designated by the home team.

*Note: It is recommended that someone other than team personnel perform this function.*

Before the game, the referee shall instruct the timekeeper as to his or her duties. The referee shall arrange with the timekeeper an understandable series of signals covering timeouts (including television timeouts), substitutions, termination of playing periods and out of bounds.

The timekeeper shall control the timing device. In the event that the official timing device malfunctions or there is no electronically controlled scoreboard clock visible to both benches and spectators, the referee on the field shall become the timekeeper.

The timekeeper shall be responsible for managing the timing sheet and the clock:

a. It is recommended that a pregame timing sheet be used in pregame administration for both regular season and postseason contests. Language that needs to be included in the regular timing sheet is: At 15 minutes, game rosters should be exchanged. At 10 minutes, captains and officials meet and teams clear the field. Officials, coaches and players are introduced. National anthem is played, if applicable. At 0:00, game begins.

## Sample Timing Sheets

## NCAA Regular Season Pregame Schedule

| *Clock* | *Activity* |
|---|---|
| 60:00* | Teams may begin warm-up. |
| 15:00 | Game rosters exchanged. |
| 10:00 | Captains and officials meet. |
| | Teams clear field. |

Introduction of officials, coaches and players.
1. Officials.
2. Visiting coaches and team.
3. Home coaches and team.

National anthem.

0:00 Game begins.

**Overtime Procedure**

| | |
|---|---|
| 5:00 | Intermission following regulation time. |
| 10:00 | First overtime period (sudden victory). |
| 2:00 | Intermission. |
| 10:00 | Second overtime period (sudden victory). |

## NCAA Postseason Pregame Schedule

| *Clock* | *Activity* |
|---|---|
| 60:00* | Teams may begin warm-up. |
| 20:00 | Captains and officials meet. |

*Begin clock 60 minutes prior to game starting time.

| | |
|---|---|
| 15:00 | Game rosters submitted and exchanged. |
| 10:00 | Teams clear field. Public address welcome. |

Introduction of officials, coaches and players.
1. Officials. (In center circle)
2. Visiting team nonstarters, followed by starters. (All to midfield, in front of bench)
3. Home team nonstarters, followed by starters. (All to midfield, in front of bench)

National anthem.

0:00 Game begins.

45:00 Kick-off • First half

Halftime 15:00 Start immediately as teams exit field

0:00/45:00 **Kick-off • Second half**

**Overtime Procedure**

| | |
|---|---|
| 5:00 | Intermission following regulation time. |
| 10:00 | First overtime period (sudden victory). |
| 2:00 | Intermission. |

10:00 Second overtime period (sudden victory).
5:00 Intermission
Penalty Kick Procedure

b. Keep track of playing time;
c. Stop the clock:
   (1) When signaled by the referee to do so:
      (a) For a television timeout,
      (b) Because a player has been instructed to leave the field for an equipment change,
      (c) To assess a player's injuries,
      (d) Because a player has been instructed to leave the field for a jewelry violation,
      (e) When a substitute(s) is beckoned onto the field in the final five minutes of the second period only; and
      (f) Because a trainer or other bench personnel is beckoned onto the field.
   (2) When a goal is scored,
   (3) When a penalty kick is awarded, or
   (4) When a player is carded;
d. Start the clock when the ball is put into play;
e. Signal the referee when a substitution is to be made, provided the ball is not in play. Signaling should be made by a noise-producing instrument with a distinctly different tone (a horn is suggested) from the referee's signaling device;
f. Call out audibly to the nearest official, if at the timekeeper's table located between the team benches, or call out over the public-address system, if time is being kept in the press box, the last 10 seconds of playing time in any period and signal for the termination of the period; and
g. Signal with a horn (not whistle) when time has expired.

*Note: The expiration of time is the moment when the timekeeper's signal starts, regardless of the position of the ball.*

**A.R. 61.** Is the timekeeper subject to jurisdiction of the referee? RULING: Yes.

**A.R. 62.** May the referee dispense with using the timekeeper and keep time on the field in the event of a timing device malfunction or in the event there is no electronically controlled scoreboard clock visible to both benches and spectators? RULING: Yes.

**Scorekeeper**

SECTION 4. There shall be one official scorekeeper designated by the home team.

*Note: It is recommended that someone other than team personnel perform this function.*

The official scorekeeper shall record team lineups, player substitutions and names of the referees and assistant referees assigned to the game. The scorekeeper shall record team scores, shots, goalkeeper saves, cautions and ejections, penalty kicks, corner kicks, goals and assists, offside, fouls and infractions, forfeitures, date, weather/field conditions, attendance, suspended games, team names and team records.

In addition, the official scorekeeper shall obtain the referee's signature on the official NCAA box score form or an 8½ x 11-inch computer-generated scoresheet with complete game information after the game is completed, thus verifying cards issued, ejection reports and the official score of the game. This shall become the official record of the game.

When required, the scorekeeper shall file scoresheets with the governing sports authority (see page 8).

**Ball Persons**

SECTION 5. It is recommended that at least four ball persons be provided by the home institution. Each ball person's duty shall be to act as a ball retriever to avoid delay of the game. All ball persons shall be instructed by and are under the direct supervision of the game officials.

Moreover, if ball persons are provided, there shall be at least four ball persons, appropriately positioned, available for the duration of the game, and they shall be at least 10 years of age.

*Note: Rule 6-5 is an administrative rule and may be altered by prior written mutual consent.*

# RULE 7

# Duration of the Game

## Length of Game

SECTION 1. The duration of the game shall be two periods of 45 minutes. For live telecasts, a timeout that may not exceed two minutes in length may be taken after the 23rd minute of each half before a throw-in near the halfway line of the field or before a goal kick.

The following procedures shall be used when a game is tied after the regulation 90 minutes.

*Note: Play shall be extended beyond the expiration of any period, in regulation time or overtime, to permit a penalty kick to be taken.*

a. For regular season, postseason, conference tournaments, play-ins and NCAA tournament games, two, sudden-victory overtime periods of 10 minutes each shall be played. A coin toss called by the visiting team will determine choice of ends of the field or the kickoff before the start of the first sudden-victory overtime period. Teams shall change ends of the field to start the second sudden-victory overtime period. If the score still is tied at the end of the second sudden-victory overtime period, the game will remain a tie for all purposes.

b. For postseason games, which include conference tournaments, play-ins and NCAA tournament games, two sudden-victory overtime periods of 10 minutes each shall be played. If the score still is tied, the game shall be recorded as a draw and the tiebreaker procedure of taking kicks from the penalty-kick line or spot, as set forth below, shall be used to determine advancement. The winner of the penalty kicks during the national championship game only will be declared the winner for all purposes, including the record.

   (1) Only players who are listed on the official NCAA game roster form shall be eligible to participate in the tiebreaker. Each team shall designate either: (a) 10 different kickers, one of whom may be the goalkeeper, or (b) 10 different kickers and a goalkeeper who will not participate as a designated kicker in the tiebreaker procedure. The kicking order shall be at the discretion of the kicking team; however, once taken, the order of the designated kickers shall remain the same. If

any of the designated players, except for the goalkeeper, are ejected during the tiebreaker, the game will continue with the remaining designated players; and the opposing team, if necessary, shall have the option to reduce or adjust its kicking order to avoid being penalized or placed at a disadvantage if the No. 1 kicker from the offending team ends up kicking against the No. 10 kicker from the nonoffending team. In addition, if the designated player ejected is the goalkeeper, his or her replacement may be from any of the eligible players listed on the official NCAA game roster for that game; however, the game will continue with the remaining designated players and the opposing team must remove one of the designated kickers from its kicking order.

(2) The visiting team shall call the coin toss, the winner of which elects to kick first or last. Each team shall take an initial series of five kicks if necessary alternately. In all games except the national championship game, the team scoring the greater number of goals shall advance to the next round.

(3) If the score still is tied after each team has taken five kicks, kicks shall continue alternately in the same order until a team has one more goal in the same number of kicks.

(4) Each kick shall be taken by a different player until 10 kicks have been taken by each team. If the number of kicks goes beyond 10, the initial order of kicking shall be repeated.

(5) The nonparticipating goalkeeper shall stay on the field of play at one corner of the penalty area. All designated players except the kicker and the designated goalkeepers shall remain in the center circle.

(6) One official shall record the kicking order, and one shall administer the taking of the kicks.

(7) Once the goalkeeper is designated, he or she shall not be replaced unless injured or ejected; and his or her replacement may be from any of the eligible players listed on the official NCAA game roster for that game. Injuries leading to replacement of the designated goalkeeper must be determined by the attending physician and/or a certified trainer in concert with the governing sports authority (see page 8).

**A.R. 63.** Are coaches permitted in the center circle at the taking of kicks from the penalty line or mark? RULING: No.

**A.R. 64.** When is a game result determined a draw? RULING: All postseason games - except the national championship game – decided by the penalty kick tiebreaker is recorded as a draw and the team scoring the greater number of goals advances to the next game (see Rule 7-1-b).

**A.R. 65.** The national championship game is determined by the penalty-kick tiebreaker. How shall the game be recorded? RULING: The team scoring the greater number of goals is the champion and is credited with a win and the opposing team is charged with a loss.

**A.R. 66.** A postseason game tied after the regulation 90 minutes is suspended due to the elements or other reasons and the coaches agree to resume the game the next day to determine the advancing team. RULING: Illegal. The game must be replayed in its entirety according to the rules of conduct. Conduct rules shall not be changed by mutual consent. All NCAA member institutions are required to conduct their intercollegiate contests according to these rules.

**A.R. 67.** A penalty kick is awarded, but before the clock is stopped the signal sounds denoting the end of the game. RULING: The clock shall be adjusted to the time when the penalty kick was awarded. Play shall be extended, if necessary, beyond the expiration of time until the penalty kick is completed.

**A.R. 68.** May a coach, bench personnel or referee say that if a game is tied in regulation, the game will not go into overtime? RULING: Illegal. The game shall be played according to the rules of conduct. Conduct rules shall not be changed by mutual consent. All NCAA member institutions are required to conduct their intercollegiate contests according to these rules.

## Halftime and Overtime Intervals

SECTION 2. The halftime interval shall be 15 minutes. The interval may be shortened to 10 minutes or fewer by prior mutual consent of the coaches and officials. The interval between the end of regulation play and the first overtime period shall be five minutes. The interval between the first and second overtime periods shall not exceed two minutes.

**A.R. 69.** What happens if a team is not ready to begin the second half after the allocated time expires? RULING: If there are no extenuating circumstances, the referee shall caution the coach and forfeit the game to the opposing team if the coach disregards the rule and refuses to rectify his or her actions within three minutes.

## End of Game

SECTION 3. The end of the game shall occur after time has expired and the referee has signed the Official NCAA Box Score form or left the site of the competition (see Rules 5-3-a and 6-4).

# RULE 8

# Start of Play

### Coin Toss

SECTION 1. At the beginning of a game, the visiting team shall call the coin toss. The team winning the toss shall have the choice of ends of the field or the kickoff. At the beginning of the first sudden-victory period, the visiting team shall call the coin toss and the procedures for choosing ends of the field or the kickoff as set forth above shall be followed.

### Kickoff

SECTION 2. At the referee's signal (whistle), the game shall be started by a player kicking the ball into the opponent's half of the field of play. Every player shall be in his or her half of the field, and every player of the team opposing that of the kicker shall remain at least 10 yards [9.14m] from the ball until it is kicked off. A goal may be scored directly from the kickoff.

The kicker shall not play the ball again after he or she has kicked off until it has been touched by another player.

**PENALTY—Indirect free kick.**

The game is started only when the ball is properly kicked off; that is, kicked forward. If the ball is not properly kicked forward, the ball again will be placed on the kickoff mark and properly kicked forward.

After the ball has been properly kicked off, it may be kicked in any direction.

PENALTY—**Any player who repeatedly kicks off improperly, willfully encroaches on the 10-yard [9.14m] distance or willfully moves beyond his or her halfway line shall be cautioned and, on repetition, ejected from the game.**

**A.R. 70.** On the kickoff, a player from Team A kicks the ball into play; but realizing that a teammate will not get it, the player kicks the ball a second time. RULING: Illegal play. Award an indirect kick to Team B.

**A.R. 71.** On the kickoff, the ball is passed back to a defensive player who moves forward with the ball. RULING: Illegal play. A kickoff must be kicked forward. Retake the kickoff.

**A.R. 72.** When does the game actually start? RULING: When the ball is kicked forward.

**After a Goal**

SECTION 3. After a goal is scored, the ball shall be taken to the center of the field and kicked off under the same conditions as when the game is started (see Rule 8-2), by the team against which the goal was scored.

**Change of Ends**

SECTION 4. Teams shall change ends of the field at the start of the second half, and play then shall start with a kickoff by a member of the team opposite to that of the team taking the kickoff at the start of the game. If overtime is necessary in regular and postseason-season games, a coin toss called by the visiting team shall determine choice of ends of the field or the kickoff before the start of the first overtime period. Teams shall change ends to start overtime period.

# RULE 9

# Ball In and Out of Play

### In Play

SECTION 1. The ball is in play at all other times from the start of the match to the finish, including rebounds from a goal post, crossbar or corner flagpost into the field of play. If the ball rebounds from an official when that official is in the field of play (e.g., a ball in flight strikes an official and goes directly into the goal) it still is in play.

### Out of Play

SECTION 2. The ball is out of play in the following circumstances:

a. It has wholly crossed a boundary line whether or not on the ground or in the air.
b. The game has been stopped by the referee.

### Restarts

SECTION 3. A ball out of play is put back in play in the following methods:

a. After crossing a boundary line—When the ball crosses a touch line or goal line, a throw-in, goal kick or corner kick is used to put it in play.
b. After temporary suspension of play—In case of temporary suspension of play due to an injury or any other cause and one team is clearly in possession of the ball, the game shall be restarted with an indirect free kick by the team in possession at the point where the ball was when play was suspended. Should there not be clear possession at the time play was suspended due to injury or any other cause, there shall be a drop ball at the spot where the ball was declared out of play, provided the ball is not in the goal area.

   If play was suspended with the ball in the goal area, it shall be dropped on that part of the goal area line that runs parallel to the goal line nearest to where the ball was when play was stopped. The ball is in play when it touches the ground; however, if the ball is played before it touches the ground, the referee shall drop it again.
c. Kickoff—(See Rule 8-2).

**A.R. 73.** The goalkeeper, in possession of ball, has been hurt in a goal-mouth scramble, but no foul has been committed. RULING: Stop the game and the clock, treat the injury and restart the game with an indirect free kick by the team in possession.

**A.R. 74.** Before the referee drops the ball and it touches the ground, a defending player in the penalty area strikes an opponent. RULING: If the misconduct took place inside the penalty area, a penalty kick shall not be awarded because the ball was not in play at the time the offense was committed. The game shall be restarted by dropping the ball after the misconduct has been penalized.

# RULE 10

# Scoring

*Note: Scrimmages and exhibitions do not count towards season statistics and card accumulations.*

### Method of Scoring

SECTION 1. A goal is scored when the whole of the ball has passed over the goal line, between the goal posts and under the crossbar, provided it has not been intentionally thrown, carried or propelled by hand or arm by a player of the attacking side, except as otherwise provided by these rules.

If a defending player deliberately handles the ball in an attempt to prevent a goal, it shall be scored a goal if it goes in.

**A.R. 75.** Standing on his or her own goal line, the goalkeeper catches the ball and, in attempting to throw the ball, carries the ball over the goal line. RULING: Goal, if the whole of the ball passed over the goal line, between the goal posts and under the crossbar.

**A.R. 76.** On a shot with the goalkeeper beaten, the ball strikes an outside agent (e.g., a dog) and is deflected away from the goal. RULING: No goal can be awarded. The ball has been stopped by an outside agent. Restart by dropping the ball at the point where the ball struck the outside agent, unless the event occurred inside the goal area, in which case the ball shall be dropped at the nearest point outside the goal area.

**A.R. 77.** Team A goalkeeper saves a shot and throws the ball downfield. Without anyone else touching it, the ball goes directly into Team B's goal. RULING: Goal. The throw is equal to a shot.

**A.R. 78.** Shall a goal be allowed if a defensive player, while in his or her own penalty area, handles the ball intentionally and propels it into his or her own goal? RULING: Yes.

**A.R. 79.** The referee whistles to signal a goal before the ball has passed completely over the goal line and into the goal, then immediately realizes the error. RULING: No goal. The game shall be restarted by dropping the ball at the nearest point outside the goal area.

**A.R. 80.** A player kicks the ball directly into the goal from a corner kick. RULING: Goal.

**A.R. 81.** A player kicks the ball directly into the opponent's goal from a kickoff. RULING: Goal.

**A.R. 82.** A player kicks the ball directly into the opponent's goal from an indirect free kick. RULING: No goal. Award a goal kick.

**A.R. 83.** A player kicks the ball directly into his or her goal from an indirect free kick taken from outside his or her penalty area. RULING: No goal. Award a corner kick.

**A.R. 84.** A penalty kick is taken. The ball rebounds directly from a goal post to the kicker, who then kicks the ball directly into the goal. RULING: No goal. Restart play with an indirect free kick to the opposing team, to be taken from the point where the ball was kicked a second time.

**A.R. 85.** A goal is scored. Before the kickoff, the referee finds that the scoring team had more than 11 players on the field at the time the goal was scored. What action is to be taken? RULING: The goal shall be disallowed, the offending player(s) and coach cautioned as appropriate and the game restarted with a goal kick.

## Scoring Plays

SECTION 2. For statistical purposes, the point value of scoring plays shall be two points for a goal and one point for an assist.

*Note: Rule 10-2 is an administrative rule and may be altered by prior written mutual consent.*

## Shots

SECTION 3. A shot is an attempt that is taken with the intent of scoring and is directed toward the goal.

*Note: A cross is not a shot. A cross is a long kick from a wide position into the penalty area in front of the goal. The intent of a cross is to set up a scoring opportunity for an attacking player. A goalkeeper who intercepts a cross is not credited with a save. To receive a save, the goalkeeper must have stopped a ball that otherwise would have gone into the goal (see Rule 10-6-a).*

Each shot results in one of five possibilities: a goal, a save, it hits the post, it is blocked by a defender, or it is high or wide.

*Note: Rule 10-3 is an administrative rule and may be altered by prior written mutual consent.*

## Goals

SECTION 4. An offensive player who either kicks or heads the ball into the goal is awarded a goal. The player is credited with two points for statistical purposes.

*Note: For statistical purposes, an "own goal" is not credited to any player; however, the goal shall be counted in the season totals "for" and "against" for the respective teams.*

a. When a defender kicks or heads the ball into his or her team's goal with the intent of making a pass back to a teammate or of clearing the ball out of danger, the goal is not credited to an individual, but is recorded as an "own goal."

b. An offensive player whose shot is deflected into the goal by the goalkeeper or a defender receives credit for the goal, provided the momentum of the shot carried the ball into the goal.
c. An offensive player whose pass is deflected into the goal by a defender or whose pass is mishandled by the goalkeeper and allowed to cross into the goal shall receive credit for a shot and a goal, provided the momentum of the shot carried the ball into the goal.

*Note: Rule 10-4 is an administrative rule and may be altered by prior written mutual consent.*

**Assists**

SECTION 5. An assist is awarded for a pass leading directly to a goal. No more than two assists may be credited on any one scoring play. Players receiving assists are credited with one point for statistical purposes.

a. If a scoring play consists of two consecutive passes without a defender gaining control of the ball, two assists may be awarded, provided the second player does not have to elude a defender to make the final pass. Both passes must have a direct influence on the outcome of a goal scored. If the second player needs to elude a defender before passing to the goal-scorer, credit only that assist.
b. No assist is awarded when a player gains control from the defensive team and scores.
c. No assist is awarded on a penalty-kick goal.
d. A corner kick, throw-in or free kick leading to a goal each counts as a pass in awarding assists.
e. A player cannot receive credit for an assist on a goal that the player also scores.
f. If an attacking player's shot hits a post or crossbar and bounces back into the field of play and, before a defender can touch the ball, another attacker shoots the ball into the goal, credit the player whose shot hit the post or crossbar with an assist.
g. If an attacking player shoots and the goalkeeper or defender blocks the shot but cannot control the ball, and a second attacking player immediately knocks the rebound in for a goal, credit the player who took the first shot with an assist.

*Note: Rule 10-5 is an administrative rule and may be altered by prior written mutual consent.*

**Goalkeeper Saves, Shutouts**

SECTION 6. a. A save is awarded to a goalkeeper only if a shot otherwise would have gone into the goal. A goalkeeper can be credited with a save without catching the ball. If the goalkeeper blocks the ball or punches it wide or over the goal, that goalkeeper can be credited with a save, provided the ball would otherwise have gone into the goal. To receive a save, the play must be a shot. A goalkeeper cannot receive credit for a save on a cross.

b. When a game is tied after regulation and overtime periods, and a penalty-kick situation determines a winner, each goalkeeper will be charged only with goals allowed prior to the penalty-kick procedure.
c. A goalkeeper is credited with a shutout only if he or she plays the entire match. If two or more goalkeepers participate in a game where no goals are allowed, no individual shutout is recorded.

**A.R. 86.** The score is tied 1-1 at the end of regulation and two overtimes. Team A wins the penalty-kick tiebreaker, 3-2. RULING: Goalkeepers for Team A and Team B are charged with one goal allowed.

*Note: Rule 10-6 is an administrative rule and may be altered by prior written mutual consent.*

### Winning the Game, Game-Winning Goals

SECTION 7. The team scoring the greater number of goals shall be designated the winner. During the regular season, if no goals or an equal number of goals are scored, the game shall be termed a "draw."

In all postseason games - except the national championship game - where the tiebreaker procedure described in Rule 7-1-b is used, the game shall be recorded as a draw and the team that wins the penalty-kick tiebreaker shall advance to the next game.

*A game-winning goal for statistical purposes is the goal that is one more than the opposing team's final total.*

### Forfeited Games

SECTION 8. The score of a forfeited game shall be 1-0. All normal statistics are nullified; however, cautions or ejections occurring in a forfeited game shall be subject to the procedures stated in Rules 5-5-b, 12-16, 12-17 and 12-18.

### Suspended Games

SECTION 9. A suspended game is considered a temporary action (because of elements or other causes). If the conditions leading to a suspended game persist and the game is not resumed the same day, the game shall be considered "no contest" if it hasn't progressed to 70 minutes. A "no contest" does not count, and all normal statistics are nullified; however, cautions or ejections occurring in a "no contest" shall be subject to the procedures stated in Rules 5-5-a, 12-16, 12-17 and 12-18.

**A.R. 87.** Due to lightning, the referee suspends a game midway into the second half of play. The storm persists, and the game cannot continue. How should the referee report the game? RULING: If the game has progressed to 70 minutes (e.g., 70:00) the referee shall report that it was suspended.

**A.R. 88.** A game is suspended at 47:47. What is the status of the game? RULING: No contest.

**Lightning Safety Policy**

SECTION 10. The purpose of this policy is to provide information to those responsible for making decisions about suspending and restarting games based on the presence of lightning.

The current recommendation of the National Severe Storms Laboratory (NSSL) is to consider terminating play when the lightning is six miles away (flash-to-bang time of 30 seconds or less). This recommendation was developed as a practical way to make a judgment in situations where other resources such as technology and instrumentation are not available.

As a minimum, NSSL staff strongly recommends that by the time the flash-to-bang count is 30 seconds all individuals should have left the game site and reached a safe structure or location.

In addition, a smaller, but still real, risk exists with the presence of lightning at greater distances. Unfortunately, current science cannot predict where within the radius the next strike will occur.

The existence of blue sky and the absence of rain are not protection from lightning. Lightning can, and does, strike as far as 10 miles away from the rain shaft. It does not have to be raining for lightning to strike.

The flash-to-bang method is the easiest and most convenient way to estimate how far away lightning is occurring. Thunder always accompanies lightning, even though its audible range can be diminished because of background noise in the immediate environment and its distance to the observer. To use the flash-to-bang method, count the seconds from the time the lightning is sighted to when the clap of thunder is heard. Divide this number by five to obtain how many miles away the lightning is occurring.

When considering resumption of a game, NSSL staff recommends that everyone ideally should wait at least 30 minutes after the last flash of lightning or sound of thunder before returning to the field of activity.

If available, electronic detection devices should be used as additional tools to determine the severity of the weather. However, such devices should not be used as the sole source when considering terminating play.

(Information taken from the NCAA Sports Medicine Handbook and NCAA Championships Severe Weather Policy).

# RULE 11

# Offside

### Offside Position

SECTION 1. A player is in an offside position if he or she is nearer to the opponent's goal line than the ball, unless:

a. The player is in his or her own half of the field of play, or
b. The player is not nearer to the opponent's goal line than at least two opponents.

### When Offside

SECTION 2. A player shall be declared offside and penalized for being in an offside position only if at the moment the ball touches or is played by a teammate, the player is, in the opinion of the referee, involved in active play by:

a. Interfering with play or with an opponent, or
b. Gaining an advantage by being in that position.

**PENALTY—Indirect free kick from the point of the infraction.**

When a player is in an offside position, that player shall not interfere with an opponent or with the play; that is, to station himself or herself so near the goalkeeper or any other opponent as to hamper the opponent's movements or obstruct his or her sight of the ball.

**A.R. 89.** Is a player offside when the ball hits the goalkeeper, one of the goal posts or crossbar and rebounds into the field of play? RULING: No. A player shall be judged offside at the moment the ball is played (i.e., kicked) and then only if in an offside position and also judged as either intending to interfere with play or an opponent, actually interfering with play or an opponent or gaining an advantage by being in that position.

### When Not Offside

SECTION 3. A player shall not be declared offside by the referee under the following situations:

a. Merely because of being in an offside position, or
b. If the player receives the ball directly from a goal kick, corner kick or throw-in.

**A.R. 90.** Shall a player be called offside when a defensive player deliberately steps off the field of play? RULING: No, the defensive player shall be cautioned for unsporting conduct (see Rule 3-6).

**A.R. 91.** A player receives the ball from a throw-in clearly in an offside position, shoots the ball and scores. RULING: Goal. A player cannot be offside on a throw-in.

**A.R. 92.** Can a player be offside when a free kick is taken? RULING: Yes, in accordance with Rule 11-2.

**A.R. 93.** Is it an offense to be in an offside position? RULING: No, it only becomes an offense at the moment the ball is played, as stated in Rule 11-2.

**A.R. 94.** An offensive player steps off the field to avoid being offside. RULING: No penalty if the player left the field for the sole purpose of not being offside. If, upon leaving the field, the player distracts an opponent or assists a teammate, the player is guilty of an infraction (see Rule 3-6).

**A.R. 95.** May a player in an offside position be penalized for being offside on a shot by a teammate? RULING: Only if the referee judges that the player in the offside position is interfering with play or an opponent, or is gaining an advantage by being in that offside position at the moment the ball is played.

## DIAGRAMS ILLUSTRATING POINTS IN CONNECTION WITH

# OFFSIDE

 –Players attacking goal.  –Players defending goal.

### OFFSIDE—Diagram 1

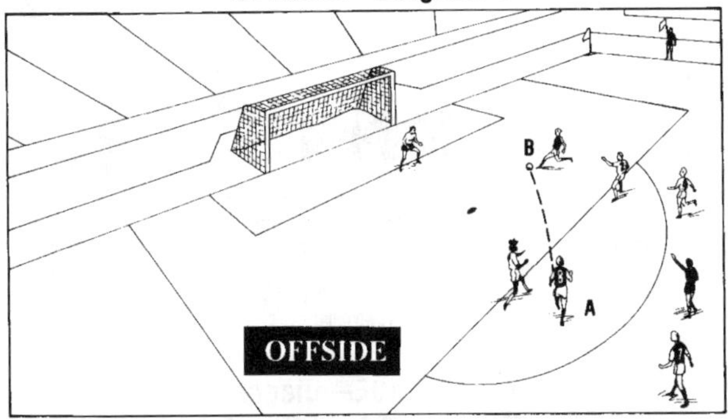


**Pass to a Teammate**

**A** passes the ball to **B**. **B** is offside because he is in front of **A** and is closer to his opponents' goal line than at least two of his opponents when the ball was passed by **A**.

### OFFSIDE—Diagram 2

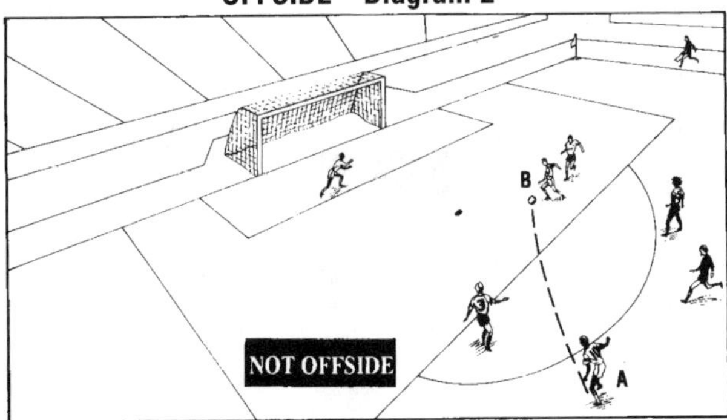


**Pass to a Teammate**

**A** plays the ball forward to **B**, who is level with the second-to-last defender. **B** is not offside since, at the moment the ball was played by **A**, she was not closer to her opponents' goal line than at least two opponents.

## OFFSIDE—Diagram 3

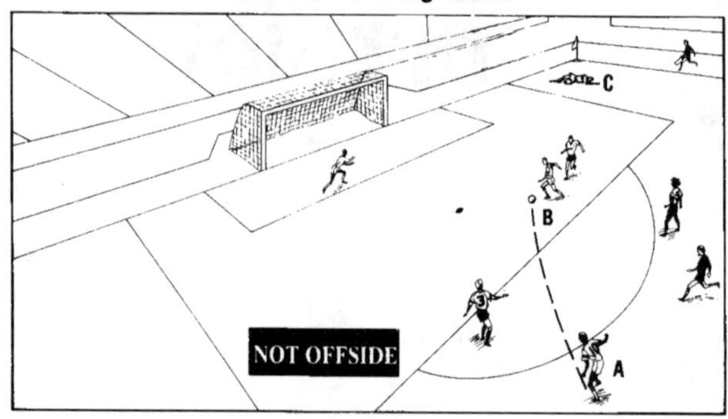


**Pass to a Teammate**

**A** plays the ball forward to **B**, who is level with the second to last defender. **B** is not offside since, at the moment the ball was played by **A**, he was not closer to his opponents' goal line than at least two of his opponents. **C**, lying injured outside the penalty area, is in an offside position but shall not be penalized since he is not involved in active play.

## OFFSIDE—Diagram 4

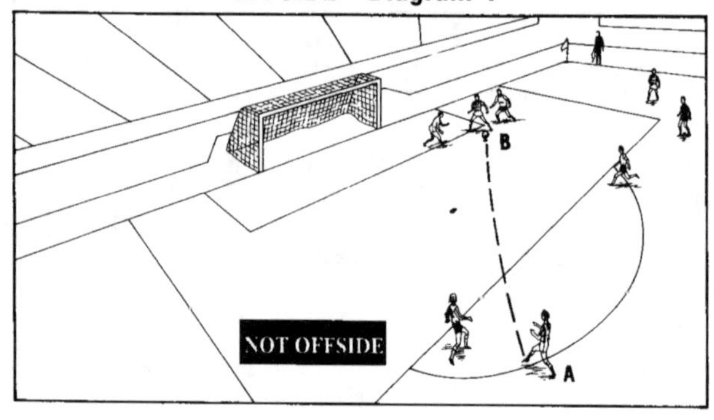


**Pass to a Teammate**

**A** plays the ball to **B**, who is level with the last two opponents. **B** is not offside since, at the moment the ball was played by **A**, she was not closer to her opponents' goal line than at least two opponents.

## OFFSIDE—Diagram 5

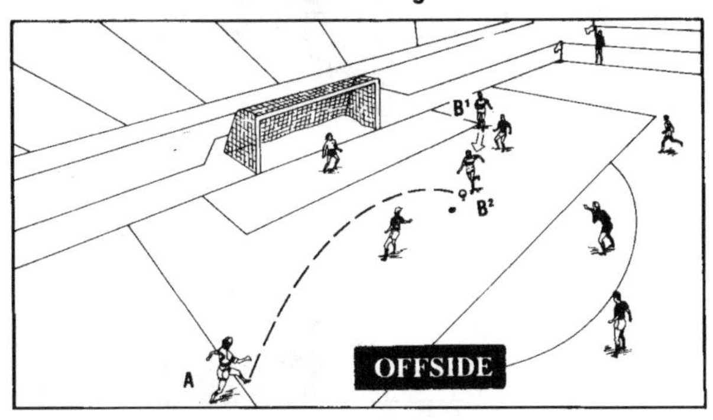


**Pass to a Teammate**

**A** crosses the ball forward from outside the penalty area. **B** runs from Position 1 and collects the ball as it lands at Position 2. **B** is offside since, at the moment the ball was played by **A**, he was closer to his opponents' goal line than at least two of his opponents and gained an advantage by being in active play.

## OFFSIDE—Diagram 6

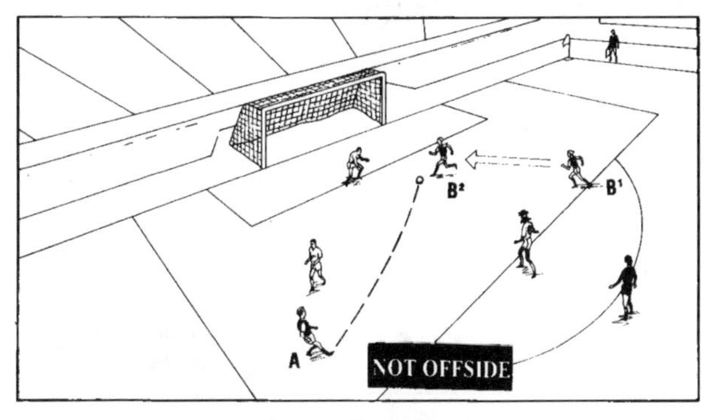


**Pass to a Teammate**

**A** passes the ball to **B**, who runs from Position 1 to Position 2 to play it. **B** is not offside because at the moment the ball was played by **A**, she was not in an offside position since she was not in front of the ball and was not closer to her opponents' goal line than at least two opponents.

## OFFSIDE—Diagram 7

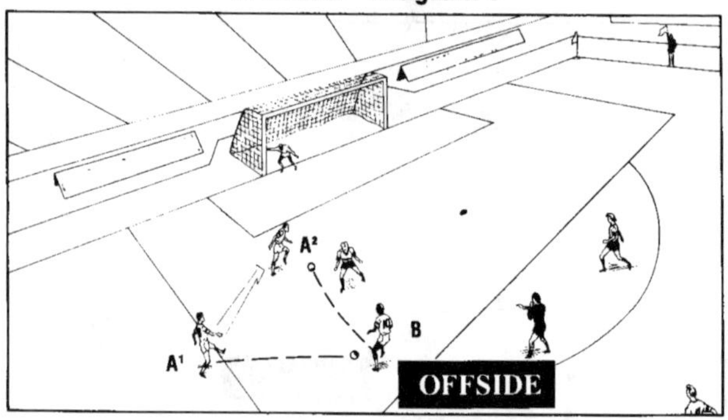


**Interpasing with a Teammate**

**A** plays the ball to **B** from Position 1 and runs forward to receive the return pass. **B** plays the ball to A, who is now in Position 2. **A** is offside since at the moment the ball was played forward to him by **B**, he was closer to his opponents' goal line than at least two opponents and gained an advantage by being in active play.

## OFFSIDE—Diagram 8

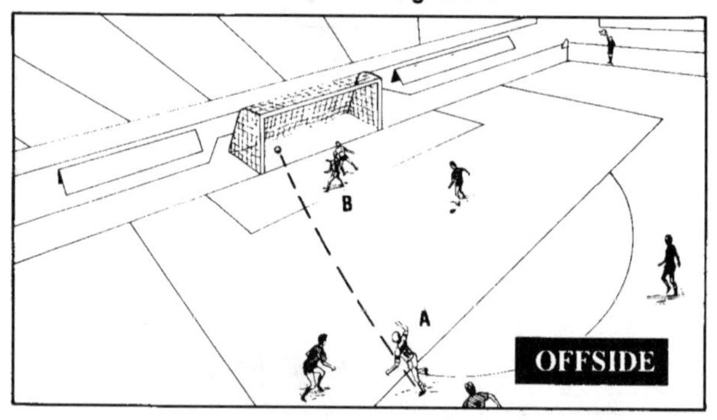


**Interfering with an Opponent**

**A** shoots for goal and the ball enters the net. **B** is standing in front of the goalkeeper. The goal shall not be allowed since **B**, who is in an offside position, is involved in active play and is interfering with an opponent.

## OFFSIDE—Diagram 9

**Shot at Goal**

**A** shoots for goal and scores. Although **B** is in an offside position, she is not involved in active play and the goal shall be allowed.

## OFFSIDE—Diagram 10

**Ball Rebounding from Goal Posts or Crossbar**

**A** shoots for goal and the ball rebounds from the post to **B**, who kicks the ball into goal. The goal shall be disallowed since **B**, who was in an offside position when the ball was last played by **A**, was in active play and gained an advantage by being in that position.

## OFFSIDE—Diagram 11

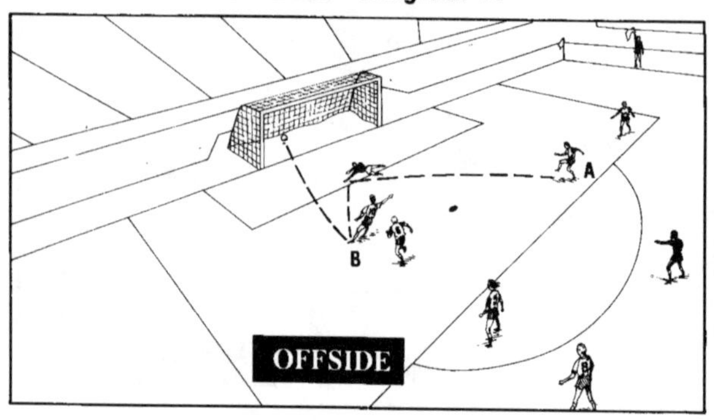


**Shot Rebounds from Goalkeeper**

**A** shoots the ball at goal and the ball rebounds from the goalkeeper to **B**, who kicks the ball into goal. The goal is disallowed since **B**, who was in an offside position when the ball was last played by **A**, was in active play and gained an advantage by being in that position.

## OFFSIDE—Diagram 12

**Not Interfering with an Opponent**

**A** shoots for goal and scores. Although **B** is lying injured in an offside position, he is not involved in active play. The goal shall be allowed.

## OFFSIDE—Diagram 13

**Interfering with an Opponent**

**A** shoots for goal and the ball enters the net. **B**, who is lying injured in the goal area and in the path of the ball, shall be penalized for offside. By her presence, however accidental, she is involved in active play and is interfering with an opponent.

## OFFSIDE—Diagram 14

**Corner Kick**

**A** takes a corner kick, and the ball goes to **B**. **B** shoots for goal and the ball is touched by **C** and enters the goal. The goal is not permitted since **C** was in front of the ball and there were not at least two opponents between him and the goal line when it was last played by **B**.

## OFFSIDE—Diagram 15

**Corner Kick**

A corner kick is taken by **A** and the ball goes to **B**, who scores. Although **B** has only one opponent between her and the goal line, the goal is allowed since a player cannot be offside if she receives the ball directly from a corner kick.

## OFFSIDE—Diagram 16

**Throw-In**

**A** throws the ball to **B**, who scores. The goal is allowed. Although **B** is in front of the ball and there is only one opponent between him and the goal line, he is not offside because a player cannot be offside if he receives the ball directly from a throw-in.

## OFFSIDE—Diagram 17

**Pass to a Teammate**

**B** plays the ball ahead of **A**, who is in her own half. Although there are not at least two opponents closer to their own goal line at the moment **B** played the ball, A is not offside since a player cannot be offside in her own half of the field of play.

## OFFSIDE—Diagram 18

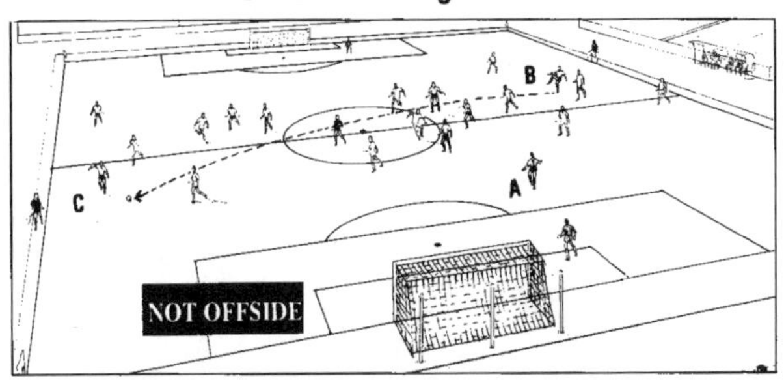


**Active Play**

The ball is intercepted by **B**, a teammate of the attacking player. It is transferred to another teammate, **C**, on the wing. Although the attacking player **A** is in an offside position, he shall not be penalized since he is not involved in active play.

**Diagrams 1-18 reprinted with permission from the U.S. Soccer Federation and the National Federation of State High School Associations.**

*No. 19. OFFSIDE–A player cannot put herself onside by running back into her half of the field of play.*

If **A** is in the opponent's half of the field of play and is in an offside position when **B** last played the ball, **A** cannot put herself onside by moving back into her half of the field of play.

# RULE 12

# Violations and Misconduct

## Violations

Spitting, Kicking, Striking, Tripping, Improper Use of Bleeding Injuries or Jumping

SECTION 1. A player shall be penalized if he or she spits, kicks, strikes, attempts to kick, strike or jump at an opponent. In addition, a player who has been injured and is bleeding or has blood on his or her uniform shall be penalized, if he or she makes intentional contact with an opponent which is otherwise avoidable.

**PENALTY—Direct free kick.**

Spitting, kicking, striking, tripping or jumping at an opponent or attempting to do the same is dangerous and liable to cause injury. In such cases, the referee shall, in addition to the stated penalty, either (1) issue a caution to the offending player if the referee considers it a misconduct and inform the player that a repetition will result in ejection from the game, or (2) eject the player immediately if the referee considers the act serious foul play or violent conduct.

*Note: Jumping at an opponent is different from jumping to play the ball.*

**A.R. 96.** An offensive player is struck by an opponent in the penalty area, but the ball is in play elsewhere on the field at the time. RULING: A penalty kick shall be awarded and the offending player shall be ejected from the game for violent conduct.

**A.R. 97.** What is the difference between a sliding tackle and tripping? RULING: For a sliding tackle to be permissible, the foot or feet shall be at or near the ground, the tackle shall be for the ball and not the opponent, the ball shall be played first and it shall be judged as not dangerous or violent.

**A.R. 98.** Is a tackle from behind permissible? RULING: Yes, only if it meets qualifications of A.R. 97 and if it is not violent with little or no attempt to play the ball.

**A.R. 99.** May a player bait an opponent into an unfair tackle? RULING: If a player deliberately turns his or her back to an opponent when he or she is about to be tackled, the player may be charged but not in a dangerous or violent manner.

### Fighting

SECTION 2. A player, coach or bench personnel shall be penalized if he or she deliberately strikes or attempts to strike another player, coach or bench personnel in a malicious manner or leaves the bench or coaching area to participate in an altercation.

**PENALTY—Ejection and multiple-game suspension (see Rule 12-16-b).**

After a fight has occurred, the referee shall inform the player(s), the head coach and the official scorekeeper that an ejection for fighting has been issued (the scorekeeper also shall note this in the scorebook).

After the game, the referee shall contact by telephone or facsimile the NISOA regional representative and inform him or her that a player(s) has been ejected for fighting.

The regional representative shall then contact by telephone or facsimile or electronic mail the athletics director of the ejected player's institution within 48 hours and inform him or her that a player(s) has been ejected for fighting.

After a fight has occurred, the referee shall inform the player(s), the head coach and the official scorekeeper that an ejection for fighting has been issued. The scorekeeper shall note the fighting ejection in the scorebook.

> After the game, the referee shall contact the NISOA regional representative by telephone and transmit by facsimile or electronic mail a completed fight reporting form.
> The regional representative shall then contact by telephone, facsimile, or electronic mail the athletics director of the ejected player's institution within 48 hours and inform him or her that a player(s) has been ejected for fighting.

**A.R. 100.** What constitutes a fight? RULING: A fight is defined as a deliberate strike or an attempt to strike another player, official, coach or bench personnel. These acts may include kicking, head-butting, hair pulling or an open-handed strike if done deliberately and in a malicious manner.

**A.R. 101.** May a coach or team representative leave the coaching area during an altercation? RULING: Yes, providing it is to restrain his or her players in an attempt to restore order.

### Handling

SECTION 3. A player shall be penalized if the player deliberately handles the ball; that is, carries, strikes or propels it with his or her hands or arms. (This does not apply to the goalkeeper within his or her penalty area.)

**PENALTY—Direct free kick.**

Inadvertent touching (the ball touching the hands or arms) shall not be penalized even though the player or the player's team gains an advantage by such inadvertent touching.

**A.R. 102.** A player takes a goal kick, it leaves the penalty area and the wind blows the ball back into the penalty area. The same player handles the ball to stop it from entering the net. RULING: Penalty kick.

### Holding and Pushing

SECTION 4. A player shall be penalized for holding, pulling the uniform or pushing an opponent.

**PENALTY—Direct free kick.**

**A.R. 103.** A player, upon being fairly charged, falls down outside the field of play but in so doing intentionally pushes or trips an opponent who is still in the field of play. RULING: Direct free kick or penalty kick if the offense occurs in the penalty area and a caution to the offending player.

**A.R. 104.** A player holds an opponent by grabbing his or her clothing. RULING: Caution the offending player and award a direct free kick or penalty kick if the offense occurs in the penalty area.

### Violent or Dangerous Charging

SECTION 5. A player shall be penalized for charging an opponent in a violent or dangerous manner.

A fair charge consists of a nudge or a contact with the near shoulder, when both players are in an upright position, within playing distance of the ball, and have at least one foot on the ground and their arms held close to the body.

**PENALTY—Direct free kick.**

### Fouling the Goalkeeper

SECTION 6. The referee shall eject without previous caution any player who, with obvious intent, violently fouls the goalkeeper who is in possession of the ball in the goalkeeper's penalty area.

**PENALTY—Direct free kick.**

**A.R. 105.** Shall a player be ejected for any type of charge upon an opposing goalkeeper? RULING: No. Whenever an opposing goalkeeper, who is in possession of the ball in his or her penalty area, is fouled in a manner that, in the opinion of the referee, is both intentional and violent, the offending player shall be ejected without caution. In all other cases, the referee shall penalize appropriately.

### Kicking Ball Held by Goalkeeper

SECTION 7. A player shall be penalized for kicking or attempting to kick the ball when it is in possession of the goalkeeper.

**PENALTY—Indirect free kick.**

### Obstruction

SECTION 8. A player shall be penalized for obstructing an opponent when not playing the ball; that is, running between an opponent and the ball or interposing his or her body as to form an obstacle to an opponent (see illustration, page 65).

**PENALTY—Indirect free kick.**

**A.R. 106.** When is obstruction not a violation? RULING: When a player places himself or herself between an opponent and the ball, keeping the ball within playing distance, and shields the ball in an attempt not to have it played by the opponent.

**A.R. 107.** How is playing distance defined when judging obstruction? RULING: By whether the player with the ball can play the ball at any given moment or if the player is preventing an opponent from playing it.

### Dangerous Play

SECTION 9. A player shall be penalized for engaging in play that is of a dangerous nature or likely to cause injury to oneself or an opponent. Some examples of dangerous play are:

a. Raising the foot to the level that may endanger an opponent when the opponent is in a normal stance;
b. Scissor kicking and bicycle kicking, which may endanger an opponent;
c. Lowering the head to a position level with or below the waist in an effort to head the ball in the presence of an oncoming player (this is likely to cause injury to the player heading the ball in such a manner); and
d. A player other than the goalkeeper covering the ball while sitting, kneeling or lying on the ground.

**PENALTY—Indirect free kick.**

**A.R. 108.** Is it permissible to play the ball while lying on the ground? RULING: Yes, provided that the player does not create a danger to himself or herself, or an opponent.

**A.R. 109.** Is the scissor kick permitted? RULING: Yes, if the act does not endanger an opponent.

## Goalkeeper Privileges and Violations

### Privileges

SECTION 10. Within his or her penalty area, the goalkeeper has certain privileges not given to any other player. These privileges include:

a. Handling–The goalkeeper may catch, carry, strike or propel the ball with the hands or arms.
b. Possession:
   (1) the act of distributing the ball after control (e.g. – dropping the ball for the kick, parrying, throwing, etc.);

OBSTRUCTION*

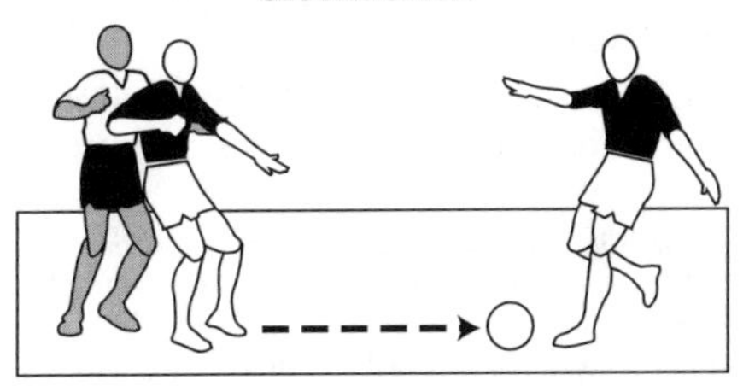

Player having made a pass to a teammate obstructs opponent to prevent him or her from tackling teammate receiving ball.

Defender having allowed ball to pass to the goalkeeper to field blocks the path of an attacker.

A player who cannot possibly play the ball because it is out of distance, moves with his or her back to opponent to prevent the opponent from reaching the ball before it goes out of play.

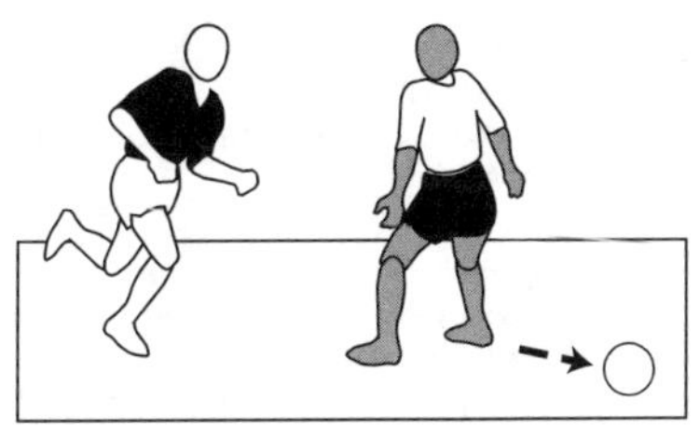

A player not attempting to play the ball is blocking the approach of an opponent who is trying to play it.

*Illustrations of Obstruction reprinted from "Know The Game—Soccer" published by Educational Productions, Ltd., London, England.

(2) tossing the ball into the air and recatching it;
(3) pinning the ball to the ground.

**PENALTY—Indirect free kick from point of infraction.**

Outside the penalty area, the goalkeeper has no more privilege than any other player.

**A.R. 110.** A player stands in front of the goalkeeper during a corner kick without trying to play the ball but merely trying to stop the goalkeeper from playing it. RULING: Illegal. Indirect free kick.

**A.R. 111.** A player raises his or her foot as the goalkeeper kicks the ball from his or her hands. RULING: Dangerous play. Indirect free kick.

**A.R. 112.** When can the goalkeeper be legally charged? RULING: When the ball is not in the goalkeeper's possession; that is, dribbled with his or her feet, but within playing distance of the goalkeeper.

**A.R. 113.** Can an opposing player ever take a position in front of a goalkeeper who is in possession of the ball? RULING: Yes, however, the opposing player who takes a position in front of a goalkeeper for the purpose of interfering with or impeding the goalkeeper shall be penalized.

## Violations

SECTION 11. With the goalkeeper's special privileges comes the capability for certain violations of these privileges that could not be applied to any other player. These violations are:

a. Six-second limit—The goalkeeper has six seconds to put the ball back into play once the individual takes control of the ball with the hands, regardless of the number of steps that are taken during this time.

**PENALTY—Indirect free kick from the point of infraction.**

**A.R. 114.** May the goalkeeper throw the ball in the air over the head of an opponent and catch it after taking more than four steps? RULING: Yes, as long as the ball is released into play within six seconds.

**A.R. 115.** A goalkeeper appears to sustain an injury while making a save while maintaining possession of the ball, during which time the six-second limitation elapses. The referee determines the goalkeeper is able to continue play. RULING: Award an indirect free kick to the goalkeeper and restart play.

**A.R. 116.** The goalkeeper throws the ball at an opponent in a vigorous manner. RULING: Caution or eject the player and award a direct kick at the point where the ball struck the player (if the player is outside the penalty area) or penalty kick, if the offense occurs in the penalty area.

b. Repossession—After releasing the ball from possession, the goalkeeper may touch or receive the ball with his or her hands only under the following conditions:
(1) The ball has been touched by a member of the opposing team, whether inside or outside the penalty area, or

(2) The ball has been touched by a member of his or her own team, providing that player is outside the penalty area and the ball has not been deliberately kicked or thrown to the goalkeeper. Further, throwing the ball into the air and allowing it to hit the ground is considered releasing the ball, and the goalkeeper may not retake possession unless the ball is touched or played by an opponent.

Parrying (e.g., a controlled deflection) shall count as possession or control. Parrying during a save or attempted save when there is no clear attempt to control the ball does not count as possession or control.

When a player deliberately kicks or throws the ball to his or her goalkeeper, the goalkeeper is not permitted to touch it with his or her hands.

**PENATY—Indirect free kick from the point of infraction.**

**A.R. 117.** A player retreating toward his or her goal with the ball passes the ball to the side of the goal, giving the impression that he or she was not seeking to pass the ball back to the goalkeeper. RULING: Illegal. In a situation where the ball is kicked by a teammate in any manner with the apparent intention of allowing the goalkeeper to take possession, the goalkeeper shall be penalized once the ball is touched by the hands.

**A.R. 118.** A teammate, while defending against a corner kick, heads the ball in the direction of the goalkeeper who receives it with his or her hands. RULING: Legal. The word "kicks" in Rule 12-11-b refers only to foot or feet.

**A.R. 119.** The goalkeeper receives a kicked ball outside the penalty area from his or her teammate, dribbles back into the penalty box and picks up the ball with his or her hands. RULING: Illegal. Penalize with an indirect kick from the point of infraction.

c. Trickery—A player may pass the ball to his or her own goalkeeper using the head, knee, chest, etc. However, if a player uses trickery in any form (e.g., flicking the ball with the foot in order to head it to the goalkeeper), the player is guilty of unsporting conduct and shall be penalized.

**PENALTY—The referee shall caution the player and award the opposing team an indirect free kick from the point of the infraction.**

## Misconduct

### Unsporting Conduct

SECTION 12. Players, coaches and team representatives are expected to conduct themselves in the tradition of fair play and sporting conduct, which is inherent in this game.

There are seven types of behavior that the referee shall penalize by caution (see Rule 12-14). There are eight types of behavior that the referee shall penalize by ejection (see Rule 12-15). Cautions and/or ejections issued during suspended, terminated or forfeited games shall stand as a matter of record.

### NCAA Tobacco Policy

SECTION 13. In accordance with NCAA Bylaws 11.1.7 and 17.1.12, the use of tobacco by student-athletes, or team or game personnel (e.g., coaches, trainers, managers and game officials) is prohibited in all sports during practice and competition.

Any student-athlete, or team or game personnel who uses tobacco during practice or competition shall be disqualified for the remainder of that practice or competition.

During regular-season play, it is the responsibility of each institution to enforce the rule for its own student-athletes, and team and game personnel. During postseason play, which includes conference tournaments, play-ins and NCAA tournament games, the governing sports authority or the games committee shall enforce the rule.

### Cautions

SECTION 14. A caution is a formal disciplinary action requiring specific procedures to be followed that include the display of a yellow card. Any player, coach, team official or participant listed on the official roster who violates the rules of conduct may be cautioned. A player shall be cautioned by the referee if the player:

a. Joins the team after the kickoff and leaves or returns to the field of play (except through the normal course of play) without first reporting to the referee or assistant referee (see Rule 5-6, A.R. 50);
b. Persistently infringes upon any of the rules of the game;
c. Shows dissent by word of mouth or action to decisions made by the referee;
d. Uses profane language in an incidental manner;
e. Engages in other acts of unsporting conduct, including taunting, baiting or ridiculing another player, bench personnel or officials;
f. Delays the restart of play; or
g. Fails to respect the required distance when play is restarted with a corner kick or free kick.

Players, coaches or team personnel who already have received a caution during the course of a game and then commit a second offense shall be ejected.

**PENALTY—Indirect free kick, or direct free kick from the point of infraction (penalty kick, if appropriate) in case of persistent infringement or unsporting conduct where the violation requires such penalty.**

**A.R. 120.** A player asks to leave the field; and, as the player is walking off the field, the ball comes toward the individual, who scores a goal. RULING: The player shall be cautioned, the goal nullified, and the game restarted with an indirect free kick by the opposing team from the place where the infringement occurred.

**A.R. 121.** A player enters or returns to the field of play without receiving approval from the referee and, apart from this, commits another more serious infringement. RULING: The player shall be cautioned for entering or returning to the field without approval and ejected for the more serious infringement.

**A.R. 122.** Players of either team are wasting time in the waning minutes on throw-ins and goal kicks. RULING: The referee has the authority to stop the clock and caution the offending players for unsporting conduct.

**A.R. 123.** The defensive team is guilty of delaying tactics by not giving the required 10 yards. RULING: Stop the clock and caution the appropriate player(s).

**A.R. 124.** A player(s) kicks the ball away to prevent the opposing team from executing a free kick. RULING: The referee shall stop—or reset—the clock, administer a caution to the offending player(s) and allow the offended team the opportunity to put the ball in play.

**A.R. 125.** A player misses a shot and uses incidental profanity directed at no one in particular. RULING: The referee shall caution the player.

**A.R. 126.** Is encroachment a form of misconduct? RULING: Yes. The referee has the authority to caution and eject on recurrence the offending player(s).

**A.R. 127.** A referee is about to caution a player but before doing so, the player commits another offense that merits a caution. RULING: Caution the player on the first offense and eject the player on the second offense.

**A.R. 128.** Play is suspended to caution a nonparticipating player for misconduct committed while the ball was in play. RULING: The game shall be restarted by an indirect free kick, against the offending player's team, given from the point where the ball was when the infraction occurred.

## Ejections

SECTION 15. An ejection is a formal disciplinary action requiring specific procedures to be followed that include the display of a red card. An ejection also requires that a misconduct report be written by the referee and submitted to the governing authority (see page 8). Any player, coach, team official or participant listed on the official roster who violates the rules of conduct may be ejected. The referee shall eject from the game a player, who cannot be replaced, a coach or any team representative if that individual:

a. Is guilty of serious foul play;
b. Is guilty of violent conduct;
c. Fighting;
d. Spits at an opponent or any other person;

e. Denies the opposing team a goal or an obvious goal-scoring opportunity by deliberately handling the ball (this does not apply to a goalkeeper within his own penalty area);
f. Denies an obvious goal-scoring opportunity to an opponent moving towards the player's goal by an offense punishable by a free kick or a penalty kick;
g. Uses abusive, threatening, or obscene language or engages in such behavior or conduct; or
h. Receives a second caution in the same match.

**PENALTY—Indirect free kick from the point of infraction, or direct free kick from the point of infraction (penalty kick, if appropriate) in case of serious foul play.**

**A.R. 129.** May a player be ejected from the game without having been previously cautioned? RULING: Yes, when the player is guilty of violent conduct, serious foul play, fighting, or is abusive in language or gesture.

**A.R. 130.** Shall a game be suspended immediately to caution or eject? RULING: No, if the referee applies the advantage clause, he or she shall caution or eject when play is suspended.

**A.R. 131.** What is the difference between violent conduct and serious foul play? RULING: The commission of any of the "direct free kick" fouls while the ball is in play in a manner judged by the referee as meriting immediate ejection without prior caution is defined as serious foul play. Any other act judged as violent by the referee is defined as violent conduct.

**A.R. 132.** May the referee eject a player, coach or other bench personnel who dissents? RULING: No, not if it is a first occurrence.

**A.R. 133.** If the referee believes that a player, coach or other bench personnel uses abusive, threatening or obscene language/gestures unintentionally, may the referee decide not to eject the individual? RULING: No.

**A.R. 134.** Is it possible to eject, without previous caution, a player for intentionally handling the ball? RULING: Yes. If a player, other than a goalkeeper within his or her penalty area, intentionally stops an opponent's obvious goal-scoring opportunity by handling the ball, that player shall be ejected.

**A.R. 135.** How shall a player be penalized who destroys an opponent's obvious goal-scoring opportunity by committing an offense punishable by a free kick or a penalty kick? RULING: The player shall be ejected. (See Rule 12-15-e.)

**A.R. 136.** Two players of the same team commit unsporting or violent conduct toward each other on the field of play. RULING: The players shall be cautioned or ejected from the game, and the game shall be restarted with an indirect free kick.

**A.R. 137.** A defensive player strikes an offensive player in the penalty area before a free kick is taken. RULING: Eject the defensive player. Do not award a penalty kick. The infringement occurred when the ball was out of play and the game shall be started with the original free kick.

**A.R. 138.** Can a player be cautioned and/or ejected during an interval between periods or after the completion of a match? RULING: Yes. Moreover, if time remains and the player in question has not been substituted for before the incident occurs or the penalty has been assessed, the team shall play short for the remainder of the game.

## Ejections and Player Eligibility

SECTION 16. a. An ejected player cannot be replaced and shall not compete in the next regularly scheduled game including postseason games or, if the offense occurs in the final game of the season, in the first scheduled game of the next season. Further, a player(s) serving a game suspension(s) shall be restricted to the designated spectator areas and prohibited from any communication or contact, direct or indirect, with the team, coaches and/or bench personnel from the start of the contest to its completion–including all overtime periods. (See Rule 12-17 and 12-18-a.) Any player receiving a second red card in the same season shall not compete in the next two regularly scheduled games, including postseason games. Moreover, any subsequent red card received by that player will require him or her to miss the next two regularly scheduled games, including postseason games. Scrimmages and exhibition games, scheduled or unscheduled, do not qualify as games with reference to ejected players.

b. A player involved in a fight shall be ejected from the game and is required to sit out the following two games, including postseason games. A player involved in a second fight in the same season shall be ejected from the game and shall not compete for the remainder of the season, including postseason games. If the first fighting offense in a season occurs after any nonfighting ejection, the fighting offense, along with the necessary two-game suspension for a previous red card, shall carry an additional game suspension (i.e., three games).

**A.R. 139.** May an ejected player sit out a rescheduled game? RULING: Yes, if the game was rescheduled before the ejection and is the next game to be played.

**A.R. 140.** Through no fault of its own, a team's regularly scheduled game is canceled by an opponent after the season begins. RULING: A substitute opponent may be added to the schedule and shall qualify as an eligible game for satisfying the games to be missed for ejected or suspended players.

**A.R. 141.** What constitutes a regularly scheduled game? RULING: Regularly scheduled games are those intercollegiate contests considered countable for team-championship selection purposes. Games against service teams, professional teams, semiprofessional teams, amateur teams, two-year colleges, club teams and four-year teams against whom competition is considered exhibition or noncountable in nature do not qualify as regularly scheduled games.

## Ejections and Coaching Staff Eligibility

SECTION 17. A coach receiving a red card shall be ejected from the game, shall leave the premises of the field of play and shall sit out the next regularly scheduled game, including postseason games. A coach serving a game suspension shall be restricted to the designated spectator areas and is prohibited from any communication or contact, direct or indirect, with his or her team, assistant coaches and/or bench personnel from the start of the contest to its completion.

If a coach coaches both a men's and women's team and is ejected while coaching a game, the coach will sit out the next game of the team he or she was coaching when the ejection occurred.

**A.R. 142.** Is a coach who is ejected from a game subject to suspension from the next game automatically as is the case with players? RULING: Yes.

**A.R. 143.** A coach or other institutional representative is ejected from the final game of the season or postseason. RULING: The coach or other institutional representative shall sit out the first game of the next season.

**A.R. 144.** A coach is ejected from the game and no other institutional representative is present to take responsibility for the management of the game. RULING: The referee shall suspend the game and submit a report to the governing sports authority. (See A.R. 54.)

## Accumulated Cautions and Game Suspensions

SECTION 18. a. Regular-season games. Any player or coach(es) who has received a total of five cautions in one season shall be suspended and shall not participate in the next regularly scheduled game, including postseason games. Each three additional cautions shall result in additional one-game suspensions. If the total is reached in the final game of the season, the player(s), coach(es) and/or bench personnel shall not participate in the first scheduled game of the next season. Scrimmages and exhibition matches, scheduled or unscheduled, do not qualify as games with reference to players suspended for accumulated cautions. Moreover, if the next regularly scheduled game is not played for any reason (and is later declared a forfeited game), the forfeited game shall not satisfy the game requirements for suspended players or coaches. If the total is reached in the final postseason game of the season, the players shall not compete in the first game of the next season. Suspended players or coaches shall serve their game suspensions in an actual contest. Further, a player(s) serving a game suspension(s) shall be restricted to the designated spectator areas and prohibited from any communication or contact, direct or indirect, with the team, coaches and/or bench personnel from the start of the contest to its completion–including all overtime periods and penalty-kick tiebreaker procedures (See Rule 12-16 and 12-17). Any game in which a suspended player or coach participates illegally shall be forfeited to the opposing team.

b. Postseason games. Caution accumulation will carry over into postseason play, which includes conference tournaments and play-ins to the NCAA tournament. Players or coaches participating in postseason play will receive a one-game suspension when a total of eight cautions have been accumulated. Further, each three additional cautions shall result in additional one-game suspensions. Moreover, if the total is reached in the final postseason game of the season, the player(s), coach(es) or bench personnel shall not participate in the first scheduled game(s) of the next season.

**A.R. 145.** A player has accumulated a total of five cautions and wishes to play in the next regularly scheduled game. RULING: Players accumulating a total of five cautions shall not compete in the next game, including postseason games.

**A.R. 146.** A suspended player participates in two or more games before being detected. RULING: The player's team forfeits all games in which he or she was ineligible to compete. However, the suspended player must serve his or her game suspension in the next regularly scheduled game, including postseason games. Actions beyond those set forth in the approved ruling (e.g., additional forfeitures, game suspensions, etc.) shall be determined by the appropriate governing sports authority (see page 8).

**A.R. 147.** A player enters a game with an accumulated total of four cautions and proceeds to receive an ejection. RULING: The player's team plays short and he or she is ineligible to compete in the remainder of the game in question as well as the next regularly scheduled or postseason game. The player also continues to carry four cautions in his or her accumulation.

**A.R. 148.** A player finishes the regular season with a total of four cautions and proceeds to receive a caution in the first postseason game. RULING: The player now has an accumulation of five cards toward eight allowable cautions inasmuch as the accumulation system allows eight for the postseason.

**A.R. 149.** A player with four cautions enters the final game of the regular season and proceeds to receive a caution. RULING: The player is ineligible to participate in the first game of the postseason.

**A.R. 150.** A player with four cautions enters the final game of the regular season and proceeds to receive an ejection. RULING: The player shall leave the game and is ineligible to compete in the first game of the postseason inasmuch as the ejection carries its own one-game suspension.

**A.R. 151.** A player receives a caution and a second card in the same game. RULING: The player shall be charged with one card (yellow) with reference to the five- or three-caution accumulation system and one card (red) with reference to the two-ejection accumulation system.

**A.R. 152.** A player enters the game with an accumulated total of four cautions, proceeds to receive a caution and then later in the game receives an ejection. RULING: Upon receiving the ejection, the player's team plays short and he or she is ineligible to participate in the remainder of the game in question as well as the next two regularly scheduled games, including postseason games (the player shall sit out one game for the ejection and another for the five-card accumulation).

**A.R. 153.** A player receives two "yellow" cards in the same game. For accumulation purposes, how many "yellow" cards does she/he have? RULING: One. It is impossible to accumulate more than one "yellow" card per game inasmuch as the second card issued to the same person in the same game shall be red.

**A.R. 154.** A player enters the postseason with one caution. How many additional cautions may he or she accumulate before a game suspension is assessed? RULING: Seven. However, a second caution in any game results in an ejection for which a one-game suspension shall be served.

**A.R. 155.** An ejected player is scheduled to serve a game suspension in the next game, which subsequently is forfeited. Does the player have to miss the next regularly scheduled game? RULING: Yes. Game suspensions shall be served with reference to actual games played.

**A.R. 156.** A player is ejected in his or her final game of postseason play. RULING: The player is ineligible to participate in the first game of the next season.

**A.R. 157.** A player has not yet served his or her penalty with reference to a rule that no longer requires such a penalty. RULING: Unless the new rule specifically states that the penalty has been rescinded, the player shall serve the penalty according to the rule in effect at the time the offense was committed.

**A.R. 158.** An ejected player or coach is serving a game suspension in a game that is suspended before it has reached the 70th minute and not resumed the same day. RULING: Since the game was not resumed the same day and is ruled "no contest," any player(s), coach(es) or bench personnel shall sit out the next regularly scheduled game, including a playoff or tournament game (See Rule 10-9).

### Nonparticipants on Field

SECTION 19. No person(s) other than the players are allowed on the field of play without permission from the referee. Trainers and coaches may enter the field only if instructed to do so by the referee.

**PENALTY—Caution or eject as appropriate and restart play by an indirect free kick from the location of the ball (if in play) at the time of the infraction.** ***Exception:*** **Nearest point outside goal area if ball was in goal area when infraction occurred.**

### Coaching from Touch Lines

SECTION 20. Coaching from the touch lines is restricted to verbal communication, without the use of aids, with one's own team and is confined to the coaching and team areas.

**PENALTY - The referee shall inform the offending coach that on a recurrence, an indirect free kick shall be awarded against the offending team from the point where the ball was when the infraction occurred. On the second infraction, a caution shall be issued. On the third infraction, an ejection shall be issued.**

**A.R. 159.** Is it permissible for a player on the field to call instructions to a teammate? RULING: Yes.

**A.R. 160.** May a coach or other bench personnel communicate (i.e., provide coaching instruction) with his/her players while attending injured player(s) while on the field? RULING: No. (see Rule 3-4-i, A.R. 19).

**Card Accumulations for Fighting**

| DESCRIPTION | PENALTY | GAMES MISSED | CARD ACCUM. |
|---|---|---|---|
| Player enters game with no cards and receives red card for fighting. | Ejected due to red card. | Remainder of the game and next two regularly scheduled games including postseason games. | One fighting red. |
| Player enters game with one red card from receiving two cards (one yellow, one red) in a previous game and receives a red card for fighting. | Ejected due to red card. | Remainder of the game and the next three regularly scheduled games including post-season games. | One fighting red, one yellow, one non-fighting red. |
| Player enters game with one non-fighting red card and one fighting red card from previous games and receives a red card for abusive language. | Ejected due to red card. | Remainder of the game and the next two regularly scheduled games including post-season games. | Two non-fighting reds, one fighting red. |
| Player enters game with one red card for fighting and receives red card for fighting. | Ejected due to red card. | Remainder of the game and season suspension including postseason games. | Two fighting reds. |

## Card Accumulation

| DESCRIPTION | PENALTY | GAMES MISSED | CARD ACCUM. |
|---|---|---|---|
| Player enters game with no cards and receives one caution (yellow). | None. | None. | One yellow. |
| Same player enters next game, receives one yellow and later, one red. | Ejected due to red card. | Remainder of the game and next regularly scheduled game, including postseason games. | Two yellows. One red. |
| Same player sits next game, returns and receives one yellow and one red. | Ejected due to red card. | Remainder of game and next two regularly scheduled games (see 12-16). | Three yellows. Two reds. |
| Same player sits next two games, returns and receives one yellow and one red. | Ejected due to red card. | Remainder of game and next two games (see 12-16). | Four yellows. Three reds. |
| Same player sits next two games, returns and receives one yellow and one red. | Ejected due to red card. | Remainder of game and next three games (two for red - see 12-16) and one for fifth yellow (see 12-18). | Five yellows. Four reds. |
| Player enters final game of regular season with three yellows and receives a caution. | None. | None. | Player has four yellows with four remaining in postseason. |
| Player who has missed one game for five-yellow-card accumulation receives one yellow card in final game of season. | None. | None. | Player has six yellow cards with two remaining in postseason. |
| Player enters postseason with one yellow card. | None. | None. | Player has seven yellows remaining. |
| Player is ejected in final game of regular season. | Remainder of game. | First game of postseason or first game of next season if team not in postseason. | Player has one red. |

# RULE 13

# Free Kicks

### Types, When Taken

SECTION 1. A free kick is taken to resume play after play has been stopped by the referee for any of the offenses listed in Sections 3 and 4 of this rule. The kick is taken by a member of the team against which the offense is committed and is taken from the point where the infraction occurred, unless otherwise specified in the rules.

Free kicks are classified either as "direct" or "indirect":

a. Direct free kick—A direct free kick is one from which a goal can be scored directly from the kick against the offending team.
b. Indirect free kick—An indirect free kick is one from which a goal cannot be scored unless the ball has been touched by a player other than the kicker before passing through the goal.

### How Taken

SECTION 2. When a free kick is being taken, no player of the opposite team shall encroach within 10 yards [9.14m] of the ball until it is in play, unless the player is standing on his or her goal line, between the goal posts. The kick shall be retaken if a player is within 10 yards [9.14m] of the ball and intentionally interferes with the kick. If a player tries to slow the game by standing or moving closer than 10 yards [9.14m] from the ball, the player shall be cautioned. If the individual repeats the infraction, that player may be ejected from the game.

As soon as the ball is in position to be played, the referee shall give a signal, which may be a whistle. The ball may be kicked in any direction. The ball shall be stationary when the kick is taken and is not in play until it has been played or touched. The kicker shall not play the ball a second time until it has been touched or played by another player.

**PENALTY—Indirect free kick from point of infraction.**

When a free kick is awarded to the defending team in the penalty area, the ball is not in play until played beyond the penalty area. The goalkeeper may not receive the ball into his or her hands from a free kick in order to thereafter kick the ball into play, or the kick shall be retaken. All opponents shall be outside the penalty area and at least 10 yards [9.14m] from the ball, or the kick shall be retaken.

Any free kick awarded to the defending team, within its goal area, may be taken from any point within the goal area.

Any indirect free kick awarded to the attacking team within its opponent's goal area shall be taken from a point on that part of the goal area line that runs parallel to the goal line nearest where the offense took place.

**A.R. 161.** On a free kick, does the attacking team also have to stand 10 yards from the ball? RULING: No.

**A.R. 162.** A player takes a direct free kick from 20 yards. The player passes the ball back to his or her goalkeeper who does not touch it, and the ball goes into the goal. RULING: Corner kick.

**A.R. 163.** A player taking a free kick inside his or her penalty area inadvertently kicks the ball into his or her goal. RULING: Because the ball did not leave the penalty area, it shall be retaken. If the ball had left the penalty area and then gone into the goal, a corner kick shall be awarded.

**A.R. 164.** On a direct free kick from 20 yards, a player takes the kick without waiting for the referee's whistle and scores a goal. RULING: Goal. A whistle is only required for the kickoff, penalty kick and whenever the referee indicates that players shall await the whistle to restart play.

**A.R. 165.** Can a direct or indirect free kick be kicked in any direction? RULING: Yes; however, kick-offs and penalty kicks shall be kicked forward.

**A.R. 166.** The ball from an indirect free kick touches an opponent and enters the net. RULING: Goal.

**A.R. 167.** Is the free kick lifted with one foot allowed? RULING: Yes, provided that in all other respects its execution does not violate the rules.

**A.R. 168.** A player takes an indirect free kick. The referee fails to give the hand/arm signal. The ball rebounds from an opponent directly into that opponent's goal. Is the goal nullified and the kick retaken? RULING: No. The absence of a hand/arm signal by the referee does not change the nature of the kick.

### Direct Free Kick Offenses

SECTION 3. Offenses for which a direct free kick shall be awarded are (see Rule 12, Sections 1 through 6):

a. Spitting at an opponent;
b. Kicking or attempting to kick an opponent;
c. Striking or attempting to strike an opponent;
d. Goalkeeper striking or attempting to strike an opponent with the ball;
e. Tripping or attempting to trip an opponent;
f. Using blood on a uniform or from a bleeding or oozing injury to assault another person;
g. Jumping at an opponent;

h. Handling the ball;
i. Handling by the goalkeeper outside the penalty area;
j. Holding an opponent;
k. Pushing an opponent;
l. Charging an opponent violently; and
m. Violently fouling the goalkeeper while in possession of the ball in the penalty area.

All direct kicks awarded to the offensive team in the penalty area are penalty kicks (see Rules 14-1 and 2).

**A.R. 169.** A direct free kick is awarded six yards inside the penalty area to the defending team and a player from the opposing team stands one yard outside the penalty area. RULING: All opposing players shall be 10 yards from the ball.

**A.R. 170.** A player takes a free kick, kicks the ball into play and then intentionally handles the ball before it has been played by another player. RULING: Punish the more serious offense by a direct free kick, or by a penalty kick if the offense took place in the penalty area.

**A.R. 171.** A player has been injured, is bleeding from the nose, mouth or other parts of the body and spits, flicks or uses blood to assault another person. RULING: Eject the player and award a direct free kick or a penalty kick if the offense took place in the penalty area.

**A.R. 172.** A player purposely rubs against an opponent with his or her blood-saturated uniform. RULING: Eject the player and award a direct free kick or a penalty kick if the offense took place in the penalty area.

### Indirect Free Kick Offenses

SECTION 4. Offenses for which an indirect free kick shall be awarded are (see Rule 12, Sections 7 through 11):

a. A player playing the ball a second time before it has been played or touched by another player at the kickoff, on a throw-in, on a free kick, on a corner kick, on a goal kick (if the ball has passed outside the penalty area) or on a penalty kick;
b. A goalkeeper holding the ball more than six seconds;
c. The goalkeeper takes more than six seconds to release the ball;
d. A substitution or resubstitution being made at an improper time;
e. A substitution or resubstitution being made without being beckoned by the referee;
f. Persons other than the players and assistant referees entering the field of play without the referee's permission;
g. Illegal or inappropriate coaching from the touch lines after previously being advised by the referee against a recurrence;
h. Dissenting by word or action with a referee's decision;
i. Unsporting behavior, including inappropriate language;

j. Dangerous play;
k. Offside;
l. Charging illegally when the ball is not within the playing distance, unless being obstructed;
m. Interfering with the goalkeeper or impeding the goalkeeper in any manner until he or she releases the ball, or kicking or attempting to kick the ball when it is in the goalkeeper's possession;
n. Illegal obstruction other than holding;
o. A player leaving the field of play during the progress of the game without the consent of the referee;
p. The goalkeeper receiving in his or her hands a ball deliberately kicked or thrown by a teammate; and
q. Use of tobacco.

*Note: An indirect free kick also is used to resume play after a player has been ejected from the game for misconduct, provided a separate violation has not been committed at the same time that requires a different ruling.*

**A.R. 173.** What is the penalty for illegal or inappropriate coaching from the touch lines? RULING: Indirect free kick from the place the ball was when the infraction was called, and upon recurrence, a caution from the referee (see Rule 12-20, 3-4-i, A.R. 19).

**A.R. 174.** A player scores a goal directly on the award of a foul for dangerous play. RULING: The penalty for dangerous play is an indirect free kick; and, if the ball goes directly into the opponent's goal, a goal shall not be given. A goal kick is awarded to the defensive team.

**A.R. 175.** What is meant by charging illegally (not violently or dangerously)? RULING: An illegal charge is one that involves a nudge or contact with the near shoulder against an opponent while the ball is in play, which is made when both players are not in an upright position, and/or not within playing distance of the ball, and/or do not have at least one foot on the ground and/or do not have their arms held close to the body.

**A.R. 176.** A player is guilty of inappropriate behavior including undesirable language, taunting, etc. RULING: The player shall be ejected.

# RULE 14

# Penalty Kicks

### When Taken

SECTION 1. A penalty kick is awarded for any infringement of the rules by the defending team within the penalty area that is penalized by a direct free kick. The ball must be in play when the infringement is committed in order for a penalty kick to be awarded.

A penalty kick can be awarded irrespective of the location of the ball if the offense by the defending team is committed within the penalty area. A goal may be scored directly from a penalty kick.

A penalty kick is not awarded for offenses that call for an indirect free kick, regardless of where or by whom the offense is committed.

### How Taken

SECTION 2. The penalty kick is taken after the referee's whistle from any place on the penalty line or spot. Only those players on the field at the time the penalty kick is awarded may take the penalty kick.

When it is being taken, all players (except for the kicker and the opposing goalkeeper) shall be within the field of play, but outside the penalty area and at least 10 yards [9.14m] from and behind the penalty line or spot.

The opposing goalkeeper, who shall remain on the goal line facing the kicker, between the goal posts, is permitted to move laterally (i.e., from side to side) but shall not step or lunge forward until the ball is kicked.

The player taking the kick shall kick the ball forward in order for it to be in play. If the ball is not put into play properly, the kick shall be retaken.

The kicker shall not play the ball a second time until it has been touched by another player. If the ball hits the goal posts or the crossbar and rebounds into play, the kicker still shall not play the ball until it has been touched by another player.

**PENALTY—If the ball is kicked a second time before it has been touched by another player, an indirect free kick shall be awarded to the opposing team and shall be taken from the spot where the infraction occurred.**

**A.R. 177.** On a penalty kick, a player of the defensive team wishes to stand off the field. RULING: No. All players, with the exception of the goalkeeper and the player taking the kick, shall stand on the field of play outside the penalty area, and at least 10 yards from and behind the penalty-kick line or spot.

**A.R. 178.** On a penalty kick, the kicker passes the ball back to a teammate who shoots and scores. RULING: No goal. The kick shall be retaken because the ball shall go forward on a penalty kick.

**A.R. 179.** On a penalty kick, the kicker kicks the ball against the crossbar and the ball rebounds to that player, who shoots and scores. RULING: No goal. Award an indirect free kick to the other team for playing the ball a second time after the ball has gone into play and before it touches or has been played by another player.

**A.R. 180.** Can a player taking a penalty kick push the ball forward for a teammate to run to it and score? RULING: Yes, provided (1) all of the players, except the player taking the kick and the opposing goalkeeper, are outside the penalty area, behind the ball and not within 10 yards of the penalty mark at the time the kick is taken; (2) the teammate to whom the ball is passed is not in an offside position when the ball is kicked and does not enter the penalty area until the ball has traveled the length of its own circumference; and (3) the penalty kick is taken in normal time.

**A.R. 181.** If a penalty kick is being retaken for any reason, may another player of the same team take it? RULING: Yes, provided the player was on the field at the time the penalty kick was awarded.

**A.R. 182.** Is a player taking a penalty kick allowed to place the ball elsewhere than on the penalty line or spot due to the waterlogged state of the field? RULING: No.

**A.R. 183.** Can a substitute be allowed to take a penalty kick in a game in which play has been extended? RULING: No, only a player who was on the field when time expired shall take the kick.

**A.R. 184.** May the player taking the penalty kick go outside the penalty area? RULING: Yes, after the signal the player may go outside the penalty area to take a longer run at the ball, though he or she cannot demand that the opponents give a clear path.

## Infringements

SECTION 3. a. On a penalty kick, for any infringement by the defending team, the kick shall be retaken if a goal has not resulted.

b. On a penalty kick, for an infringement by the attacking team other than the player taking the kick, the kick shall be retaken if a goal has resulted.

c. On a penalty kick, for any infringement by the player taking the kick committed before the ball is in play, the player shall be cautioned or ejected as appropriate, and the kick taken. For any infringement by the player taking the kick committed after the ball is in play, the player shall be cautioned or ejected as appropriate; a goal may not be scored, and the game shall be restarted with a free kick as appropriate to the disciplinary actions.

**A.R. 185.** The whistle has blown for the taking of a penalty kick; and, before the actual kick, the goalkeeper moves forward and his or her feet are no longer in contact with the goal line. RULING: Do not suspend play until after the penalty kick. If a goal is scored, the infraction shall be ignored; but if a goal is not scored, the kick shall be retaken.

**A.R. 186.** On a penalty kick, the offensive team infringes upon the rule. RULING: The kick shall be retaken if a goal is scored. If a goal is not scored and the ball rebounds into play, an indirect free kick shall be awarded against the offending team. If the ball goes out of play over the goal line, a goal kick shall be awarded.

**A.R. 187.** The player taking the penalty kick or the goalkeeper commits unsporting conduct before the kick is taken. What action should the referee take? RULING: As the ball was not in play, the referee will caution or eject as appropriate for the misconduct and order the penalty kick to be taken or retaken as appropriate.

**A.R. 188.** A player intentionally goes beyond the boundary of the field of play on a penalty kick. RULING: The player shall be cautioned and ejected from the game if he or she repeats the offense.

## End of Time Variations

SECTION 4. If the ball touches the goalkeeper before passing between the posts and completely over the goal line when a penalty kick is being taken at or after the expiration of time, it does not nullify a goal.

If necessary, play shall be extended at the end of any period of play to allow a penalty kick to be completed.

If a penalty kick is taken after the expiration of time, only the kicker and the goalkeeper may play the ball.

**A.R. 189.** A penalty kick has been awarded at the close of a period without any time remaining. When shall the period end? RULING: The extension shall last until the moment the kick has been completed, which is when one of the following occurs: (1) The moment the whole of the ball crosses the goal line; (2) The ball deflects into the goal from the cross bar and/or goal post(s); (3) The ball touches the goalkeeper and enters the goal; (4) The ball clearly is saved by the goalkeeper; (5) The ball passes over the goal line outside the goal post(s); or (6) The movement of the ball has ceased.

**A.R. 190.** When shall a penalty kick that has been awarded at the close of a period without any time remaining be retaken? RULING: (1) When the ball is stopped by an outside agent; (2) If a defending player encroaches and a goal is not scored; or (3) If a goal is scored after encroachment by a teammate.

# RULE 15

# The Throw-In

### When Taken

SECTION 1. A throw-in is taken to put the ball back into play after it has passed completely over a touch line, either on the ground or in the air (see Rule 9-3-a).

### How Taken

SECTION 2. The thrower, at the moment of delivering the ball, shall face the field of play and part of each foot shall be either on the touch line or the ground outside the touch line. The thrower shall use both hands equally and shall deliver the ball from behind and over his or her head. The throw-in shall be taken from the point where it crossed the touch line, being thrown in any direction by a player of the team opposite to that of the player who last touched the ball. The ball shall be in play from the throw as soon as it enters the field of play. A goal may not be scored directly from a throw-in.

The thrower shall not play the ball a second time before it has been touched by another player.

*Note: The player taking the throw-in may not use stickum or adhesive material of any kind (including gloves with an adhesive surface) to enhance the grip on a throw-in.*

**PENALTY—If the ball is improperly thrown in, the throw-in shall be taken by a player of the opposing team.**

**A.R. 191.** A player taking a throw-in throws the ball so that it does not enter the field of play but passes outside the touch line or hits the ground before entering the field of play. RULING: The throw-in shall be retaken.

**A.R. 192.** A player throws the ball in, and upon seeing that a teammate will not reach it, handles the ball and knocks it out of bounds. RULING: Award a direct free kick for the more serious offense.

**A.R. 193.** An opponent stands in front of the thrower and jumps up and down waving his or her arms. RULING: Caution the player for unsporting conduct.

**A.R. 194.** May a thrower take a long run before releasing the ball? RULING: Yes, provided the player is facing the field of play, has part of each foot on or behind the touch line, delivers the ball from behind his or her head and throws the ball in from the point it crossed the touch line.

**A.R. 195.** On a throw-in, the ball is thrown directly into the opponent's goal. RULING: No goal. Award a goal kick.

**A.R. 196.** On a throw-in, the ball is thrown directly into the player's own goal. RULING: No goal. Award a corner kick.

**A.R. 197.** On a throw-in, the ball lands on the touch line. RULING: The ball is in play.

**A.R. 198.** On a throw-in, the ball crosses the touch line in the air but is blown out of the field of play by the wind and lands outside the field of play. RULING: Award a throw-in to the opposing team.

**A.R. 199.** A player throws the ball against an opponent's back and plays the rebound. RULING: Legal, unless the ball is thrown at the opponent in an unsporting or violent manner.

**A.R. 200.** On a throw-in, the ball is thrown in an unsporting or violent manner against an opponent's body. RULING – Illegal; caution or eject the thrower as appropriate. Restart with an indirect free kick at the point of contact.

**A.R. 201.** Is it permissible for a goalkeeper to throw the ball into play from the touch line? RULING: Yes, since the goalkeeper may play anywhere on the field.

**A.R. 202.** When shall the ball be considered in play from a throw-in? RULING: As soon as any part of the ball touches or covers any part of the touch line, either on the ground or in the air.

**A.R. 203.** During a throw-in, may any part of each foot or both feet extend past the touch line into the field of play? RULING: Yes, providing at least some part of the leading foot touches the touch line.

**A.R. 204.** Is a throw-in taken while kneeling allowed? RULING: No.

**A.R. 205.** Is a "handspring" throw-in allowed? RULING: Yes.

### Throw-in to Goalkeeper, Violation

SECTION 3. A goalkeeper may not catch with his or her hands, a ball passed from a teammate taking a throw-in.

**PENALTY—Indirect kick from the point of contact.**

# RULE 16

# The Goal Kick

### When Taken

SECTION 1. A goal kick is taken by a member of the defending team when the ball passes completely over the goal line [except when a goal is scored (see Rule 10-1)], either in the air or on the ground, having last been touched by a member of the attacking team.

### How Taken

SECTION 2. The ball is placed on the ground at any point within the goal area and is kicked into the field of play beyond the penalty area, or the kick shall be retaken. A goal may be scored directly from a goal kick.

Players of the team opposing that of the player taking the goal kick shall remain outside the penalty area until the ball goes over the penalty-area line after the kick has been taken, or the kick shall be retaken.

The goalkeeper shall not receive the ball into his or her hands from a goal kick in order that he or she may thereafter kick it into play. The goalkeeper cannot pick up the ball and kick it—the ball must be placed on the ground and kicked from there.

The kicker may not play the ball a second time after it has passed beyond the penalty area and before it has touched another player.

**PENALTY—Indirect free kick from point of infraction.**

**A.R. 206.** A goalkeeper takes a goal kick on a muddy field, and the ball goes only six yards. The goalkeeper then picks up the ball and punts it. RULING: Illegal play. The ball must leave the penalty area. The goal kick shall be retaken.

**A.R. 207.** A player clearly is in an offside position when a ball is kicked to him or her from a goal kick, and the player receives the ball and scores a goal. RULING: Goal. A player cannot be offside directly from a goal kick.

**A.R. 208.** Rule 16-2 and Rule 13-2 seem to be in conflict. What is the difference? RULING: There is no conflict. In both instances, the ball is not in play until it has left the penalty area. On goal kicks, opponents shall not enter the penalty area until the ball leaves the area. On free kicks taken from within the penalty area by the defending team, opponents shall not enter the area and shall not come within 10 yards of the ball until it is in play.

# RULE 17

# The Corner Kick

### When Taken

SECTION 1. A corner kick is taken by a member of the attacking team when the ball passes completely over the goal line [except when a goal is scored (see Rule 10-1)], either in the air or on the ground, having last been played by a member of the defending team.

### How Taken

SECTION 2. A member of the attacking team shall take a kick from within the quarter circle at the nearest corner flagpost, which shall not be removed. A goal may be scored directly from a corner kick.

Players of the defending team shall not approach within 10 yards [9.14m] of the ball until the ball is in play, that is, has been touched or traveled forward, or the kick shall be retaken.

The kicker shall not play the ball a second time after the ball is in play until it has been touched by another player. If the ball hits the goal post and rebounds toward the kicker, that player still shall not play the ball until it has been touched by another player.

**PENALTY—Indirect free kick from point of infraction.**

**A.R. 209.** A player from Team A takes a corner kick. The ball hits the goal post and rebounds to the same player, who kicks it into the goal. RULING: No goal. Award an indirect free kick from the point the individual played the ball the second time.

**A.R. 210.** May a player remove the corner flag or marker before taking a corner kick? RULING: No.

**A.R. 211.** An offensive player, clearly in an offside position, receives the ball directly from a corner kick and scores. RULING: Goal. A player shall not be declared offside if the ball is received directly from a corner kick.

**A.R. 212.** A defensive player takes a position less than 10 yards from the ball on a corner kick. RULING: The player shall be instructed to move 10 yards from the ball. Continued infringement shall result in a caution and possible ejection from the game.

# Index to Rules

# Official Referee's Signals

# Official Assistant Referee's Signals